MASTERCLASS:
WRITING
COMEDY

Lesley Bown

Teach®
Yourself

Masterclass: Writing Comedy

Lesley Bown

First published in Great Britain in 2015 by John Murray Learning.
An Hachette UK company.

This edition published in 2015 by John Murray Learning

British Library Cataloguing in Publication Data: a catalogue record for
this title is available from the British Library.

Paperback ISBN 978 1 473 60218 2

eBook ISBN 978 1 473 60220 5

The publisher has used its best endeavours to ensure that any
website addresses referred to in this book are correct and active at
the time of going to press. However, the publisher and the author
have no responsibility for the websites and can make no guarantee
that a site will remain live or that the content will remain relevant,
decent or appropriate.

The publisher has made every effort to mark as such all words which
it believes to be trademarks. The publisher should also like to make
it clear that the presence of a word in the book, whether marked or
unmarked, in no way affects its legal status as a trademark.

Every reasonable effort has been made by the publisher to trace the
copyright holders of material in this book. Any errors or omissions
should be notified in writing to the publisher, who will endeavour to
rectify the situation for any reprints and future editions.

Typeset by Cenveo® Publisher Services.

Printed and bound in Great Britain by CPI Group (UK) Ltd., Croydon,
CR0 4YY.

John Murray Learning policy is to use papers that are natural,
renewable and recyclable products and made from wood grown in
sustainable forests. The logging and manufacturing processes are
expected to conform to the environmental regulations of the country
of origin.

John Murray Learning
338 Euston Road
London NW1 3BH
www.hodder.co.uk

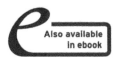

For Nicky, Rob and Kerry, because
you make me laugh

Acknowledgments

Thanks to everyone who helped with this book, and special thanks to Alan Ayckbourn, Simon Brett, Eric Chappell, Phil Collinge, Ray Cooney, Jan Etherington, Ann Gawthorpe, Mindy Glazer, Rob Grant, Candy Guard, Miranda Hart, Paul Hayes-Watkins, Sue Limb, Chris Ritchie, Ken Rock, Victoria Roddam, Robert Ross, Tony Staveacre, Count Arthur Strong, Kev F. Sutherland and Mike Vardy.

Contents

Meet the author

It started, as these things often do, innocently enough. There was a noticeboard in the main school corridor where we pinned up announcements of netball matches, choir practices and play rehearsals. I added a short humorous piece, which turned out to be the equivalent of lighting a blue touchpaper. Luckily, I was standing well back when the hordes descended. Eventually, crowd control was instigated, each group being allowed five minutes before they were moved on.

It was a pre-Internet example of viral marketing. The first reader was one of the new kids, barely tall enough to see the board, who beetled off and told her friends, so that then there were five, then ten, and by the end of the lunch break mass hysteria was breaking out.

It was a heady experience, and it also taught me something about the strange place comedy writers occupy in the world. The teachers, even before they'd wiped the grins from their faces, were at great pains to tell me that it was All Very Well Young Lady, but Real Life is a Serious Business.

Nothing has changed. I am still pinning comedy up on the metaphorical noticeboard, and I am still not serious enough for Real Life. Unreal Life, on the other hand, is a great place to be.

Introduction

> ## Charles Dickens, *Hard Times*
>
> *'People must be amuthed, Thquire, thomehow… they can't be alwayth working, nor yet they can't be alwayth learning.'*

This is not a funny book. There are plenty of funny books out there, but this isn't one of them, because comedy writing is a serious business. Mind you, the first rule of comedy writing is 'Never tell your audience that you're going to make them laugh', so perhaps this is a funny book after all, and I just don't want to tell you in case you don't laugh. The only way to find out is to read the book.

There are multiple theories about why we laugh. Is laughter a relief from repression, a safety valve for aggression, a way of bonding or a yell of victory? And is comedy a coping mechanism when times are tough, a way of cutting authority figures down to size or a way of enjoying the misfortunes of others? Is it about reinforcing shared values or about feeling superior? Why do we laugh equally at witty word play and yucky sick jokes? And why do we laugh when we're tickled? Luckily, you can write comedy without knowing the answers to these questions, although it does help to understand the basics of humour.

Most art simply doesn't survive. Jane Austen is still popular, but who now reads Fanny Burney, Mary Russell Mitford or Maria Edgeworth, who were all contemporaries of hers? Austen survives partly because she was an outstandingly good writer, but also because she chose subjects that still resonate with us today. In other words, there must be an element of luck. Just like Jane Austen, you can only write about what interests you, and there is no way of knowing who will share that interest or for how long.

Comedy is even more ephemeral than other types of art, because it is so much about what is happening now, and because it only really works if it can be grasped more or less instantly. Even the laugh that comes from a joke that needs a little thought is only a few seconds behind the punchline.

When Dorothy Parker was told that 'Calvin Coolidge is dead', she reportedly replied 'How can they tell?' This is only funny if you happen to know that Calvin Coolidge was an American President famous for his lack of small talk and his deadpan manner. Of course, the joke can be endlessly recycled but very few people now will relish the original.

You can see from the Calvin Coolidge joke that comedy often does more than just make us laugh – it tells us something about our culture. Since culture changes over time, as does how we see ourselves as a nation, comedy will also change. This matters more to some writers than others. P.G. Wodehouse somehow managed to transcend the area of British culture he wrote about, and his books are still funny today, decades after its disappearance. It remains to be seen whether the same will be true of Alan Bennett and Victoria Wood, although I sincerely hope that it is. It is certainly true that much comedy depends on shared values and shared cultural reference points.

There are also shared taboos. These are culture-specific, although some must be more universal than others. They also change over time, so what seems politically correct to us now will no doubt be all wrong in 50 years' time. Taboos are not, incidentally, anything to do with whether or not something is funny. A joke can be screamingly funny but if it's not acceptable to the audience then it won't raise a titter.

The better news is that scientists have definitely proved that laughing is good for us, and we all need to do more of it. It's quite hard to laugh at nothing, so we need comedy writers and performers to create laughter for us. One of the odd things about laughter is that we don't laugh so easily at real events. If we see someone slip on a banana skin, we rush to help them up, but we're willing to laugh at an actor doing the same thing. The world of comedy is an artificial environment in which laughter is permitted because nothing is real.

Like I said, comedy is a serious business and so, if you want to write comedy, you need to start by doing some research: consume as much comedy as you can; if it makes you laugh, work out why; and, if it doesn't make you laugh, work out why.

If anyone suggests that you're spending too much time enjoying comedy, explain that it's research.

That's the upside of comedy writing. For the downside, read this book. No, that's not quite what I meant. This isn't a funny book, but it won't be a depressing read. You'll find clear explanations of the various elements of comedy, and exercises to help you practise what you've learned. You won't find much about my personal taste in comedy. Like most people, I have strong preferences but that's not the point. There are many different audiences for many different types of comedy, and all are equally worth while.

You also won't find swearing or sexual or religious jokes in the examples offered in this book. My personal taboos may be tighter or looser than yours, but as far as possible I've tried to write a book that is accessible to everyone. Once you've learned how to do it, you can apply it to whatever kind of comedy floats your boat.

The examples are mostly taken from comedy classics, simply because most readers will already be familiar with them, and in any case they're easily accessible. The invented examples are intended to make the point rather than hit the comedy heights. Various exercises throughout the book will take you through ways of writing comedy in a series of graded steps. Work through them at your own pace, but do start at the beginning and take in all the steps, otherwise you're likely to miss something important. The exercises are as follows:

 Snapshot is a short exercise or task related to the main idea in the adjacent text.

 Write exercises – self-explanatory – ask you to write about a specific aspect of the task of writing comedy.

 Workshop exercises are longer exercises that ask you to do a bit more work – for example creating background details for your characters.

 Edit is a reworking or review of a previous piece or exercise.

When I say 'audience' in the text, I mean anyone who is on the receiving end of comedy. Whether they're in a theatre or cinema, reading a book or magazine, listening to the radio or an audiobook, or at home watching TV, they are an 'audience' as far as this book is concerned. I've occasionally used 'listener' or 'reader' where I need to be specific, but otherwise 'audience' it is.

Scattered throughout the book are key ideas and focus points related to the text, as well as quotes about comedy, most of which were very kindly given to me by other comedy professionals. You'll see from reading them that there is more than one approach to comedy writing.

Let's get started, and let's start with an exercise.

What makes you laugh?

Write down everything that's made you laugh today. Describe it in detail, and say why you laughed. If nothing made you laugh, look back to yesterday or the day before. If you have to go back more than a week, perhaps comedy writing isn't for you.

1

Comedy basics

It's pretty difficult to fake laughter: ask any actor. It's also hard to stop laughing once you've started: again, actors will tell you about the nightmare of 'corpsing' – when they break character by getting the giggles on stage and being unable to stop. It can also be just as hard to start laughing if you're not in the mood. We really don't have much control over laughing and perhaps that's why we value it so much.

So what makes us laugh? Or rather, what is there in common between the various things that make us laugh? In this chapter you will learn about the many ways of creating laughs, including surprise and recognition, and about visual, verbal and physical comedy.

Alan Ayckbourn, director and playwright

'If I had to give just one piece of comedy writing advice it would be: for God's sake take it seriously.'

Key idea

The two main factors in creating laughs are surprise and recognition.

Most laughs come from surprise: the sudden unexpected event, the twist that you didn't see coming, the moment when the penny drops. A lot of surprise laughs are created when an audience thinks they recognize what's about to happen, and are taken by surprise with what actually does happen.

We usually laugh at moments of recognition in a less explosive, more thoughtful way. It's a rueful, 'Yes, I do that too' sort of laugh. Observational comedy makes great use of recognition precisely because it is based on everyday life, but to be successful it has to include some surprises too. Recognition laughs are very useful as laughs along the way, as you build up to the big surprise punchline.

Create surprise

To practise creating surprise, have a go at this job applications exercise.

Who would be the worst possible applicants for these jobs: heart transplant surgeon, TV weather forecaster, massage therapist? There are no correct answers, but whatever you choose will only be funny if it's surprising.

Focus point

The key concept in creating both surprise and recognition laughs is incongruity, because the incongruous is also the unexpected. This works at every level of comedy, from the simplest joke to the most complex plot.

Create incongruity

To practise creating incongruity, try this simple exercise. First choose a character from list A and another from list B.

- List A: doctor, maths teacher, High Court judge, politician
- List B: used car salesman, streetwise teenager, hairdresser, plumber

Now write a short speech for one of the characters using the type of language you'd expect from the other character. For instance, the doctor could be looking at a patient's operation scar and saying 'What cowboy did this, then? I could sort it out but it won't be easy, can't get the parts you see, could fit you in Tuesday week, cash in hand all right with you, Squire?' and so on. Choose your own incongruous characters and try the exercise again. You can use specific people (such as the Prime Minister) or fictional characters (such as Robin Hood).

Creating laughs

Let's look at ways of creating incongruity, surprise and recognition in more detail, but first a couple of exercises.

What do you find funny?

Make a list of the words and objects that you personally find funny.

The more boring the better...

Write about something boringly ordinary and humdrum that you did yesterday. It could be something like travelling to work, watching TV or buying carrots – as long as nothing interesting exciting or amusing happened. Describe what you were doing and the environment you were in. Maximum 750 words.

OPPOSITES

Opposites provide instant incongruity: big and small, happy and sad, funerals and weddings. This is why double acts often exaggerate the physical differences between them; for instance, Laurel was thin and Hardy was fat. The casting of *Only Fools and Horses* must have been helped by the 20-cm (8-inch) height difference between David Jason and Nicholas Lyndhurst. Of course, sometimes this can be an illusion – neither Morecambe nor Wise was a particularly big man but much was made of Wise being the shorter of the two.

MISDIRECTION

Misdirection is when a joke or situation creates an expectation in the audience, and instead of meeting the expectation you deliver something different and surprising. It's very common in word-play jokes:

> I'm sure wherever my granny is, she's looking down on us. She's not dead, just very condescending.

INVERSION

Turning things around, or looking at them backwards, creates incongruity: for instance, a tough guy who's scared of spiders or a child with more sense than its parents.

MISUNDERSTANDING

Misunderstanding is a staple of comedy plotting. It's often thought of as primarily for farce but it is actually used all the time in sitcoms, including the classics such as *Frasier* and *Fawlty Towers*. For instance, there's an episode of *Coupling* where Jane is asked to dinner by someone she fancies and decides to snare her man by wearing nothing under her coat – and then discovers it's actually a dinner party.

 Key idea

You can get a laugh if the audience learns the truth at the same time as the character, but you can also choose to let the audience in on the secret.

A good example of letting the audience in on it is in Alan Ayckbourn's play *Absurd Person Singular*. In the second act, Eve is trying to commit suicide. The audience quickly realizes this but none of the characters does, although each time she tries they manage, without realizing, to prevent her.

EXAGGERATION

Exaggeration is an obvious comic tool but needs to be used very precisely because it has an effect on the tone of a piece. Look at the differences between Jim Carrey's exaggerated performance in *Ace Ventura: Pet Detective* and his far more subtle approach in *The Truman Show*. It's exactly the same with writing – the more you exaggerate, the broader the comedy.

DOUBLE ENTENDRE

Our appetite for double entendre, or innuendo, seems bottomless, despite the fact that we simultaneously acknowledge that it is extremely childish and not really funny at all. Of course, it's possible to create double entendres that aren't smutty but there isn't very much comedy value in those.

> ## Key idea
>
> The more censorship and repression there is, the more double entendre flourishes.

BATHOS

Bathos is the move from the sublime to the ridiculous. It's another form of exaggeration because it works by exaggerating the contrast between the two. For instance, the movie *Shaun of the Dead* takes the horror movie genre and sets it in boring suburban London rather than a spooky castle, deserted wood at midnight or other conventional horror setting.

THE RULE OF THREE

There is something about the rhythm of threes in language that really works – Faith, Hope and Charity, or Sex, Lies and Videotape. In comedy this seems to be a simple case of set-up, establishment, and punchline. So you start your list with the set-up, the second item establishes that this is a list and prepares the audience for the third item, the funny one:

> It was a very old plane. It was held together by faith, hope and chewing gum.

Or you can make all the items funny but build to the third one:

> It was a very old plane. It was held together by sticky tape, string and dinosaur sweat.

The audience will anticipate that the third element will be funny but, even so, you have to find a way to surprise them with it.

AND FINALLY...

There is a whole raft of words and objects that are perceived to be incongruous and therefore funny without any rational explanation – in other words, it's a mystery. The list changes over time and has cultural variations. Using them adds texture to your writing, although they aren't generally used in punchlines.

K is the funniest letter of the alphabet and 32 is the funniest number. Hamsters are funnier than cats, chip shops are funnier than carpet shops and so on. Sometimes analysts attempt explanation – K is a plosive consonant, 32 sounds funny in certain accents, cats are culturally perceived as elegant and intelligent whereas hamsters aren't, and so on. Mostly these feel unconvincing, and as a writer you only need to know what gets laughs.

Workshop

Take the humdrum event from the writing exercise above and consider what you could do with it to create humour. Create eight different versions, using each of the following:

- Opposites
- Misdirection
- Inversion
- Misunderstanding
- Exaggeration
- Double entendre
- Bathos
- The rule of three.

For example:

- Exaggeration – on the journey to work, so many things go wrong that you arrive when it's time to go home.
- Misdirection – describe watching a soap opera as if it were a piece of cutting-edge theatre.
- Bathos – there's a world shortage of carrots. Your dinner party is ruined.

Visual, verbal and physical

The three broad categories of comedy are visual, verbal and physical. Visual comedy is anything that creates a picture for the audience, whether it's performers carrying out actions or delivering speeches laid down in a script, or a word picture in a novel. Verbal comedy relies on word play. Physical comedy is entirely about performance.

VISUAL COMEDY

Word pictures can create jokes that would be beyond the physical capabilities of most performers or are even physically impossible. In other words, they range from the almost realistic:

I slept like a log last night. I woke up in the fireplace.

to the totally surreal:

Last night I dreamed I was eating a huge marshmallow. When I woke up the pillow was gone.

If you're writing for performance, you'll need to describe the actions and props that will produce the visual laughs, and if you're writing prose you'll need to create funny pictures to amuse your readers.

Focus point

If you're writing for performance, make sure that the actions are physically possible. Test them out yourself just in case you've written something that needs three hands to accomplish.

You'll find more about creating word pictures as you read on.

Phil Collinge, comedy writer and freelance radio producer

'There is a technique to writing good comedy, and it can be learned (which is probably why you're reading this). Having a killer wit doesn't do any harm either, of course, but if you don't know how to structure a funny line or a routine, you will struggle. So watch your heroes in action, read scripts, analyse routines... and finish this book!'

VERBAL COMEDY

Verbal jokes usually depend on some sort of wordplay, such as a pun. Although they're often clever, they're not usually screamingly funny, so they work best if they are slotted into a word picture that is also funny.

Simple wordplay is often used to create a light atmosphere, such as a hairdresser's called Hair Today or a chip shop called The Fish Plaice. A play on words can also make a joke, such as:

> A subservient fish knows his plaice.

but they're more likely to get a groan than a laugh. To get a laugh, you need a visual element:

> There's a new portable stereo on the market that looks like a chocolate cake. It's called a gateaux blaster.

You'll also find out more about verbal comedy as you read on.

PHYSICAL COMEDY

Physical comedy is ancient, accessible and transcends language. It's easy to assume that there isn't much call for writers of physical comedy – isn't it up to the performer to just go out there and be funny? However, when I tell you that there are three writers listed for *Mr Bean*, you'll understand that someone has to think up all that funny business. Writers of physical comedy can expect to work in close collaboration with the performers, who will each have their individual abilities and limitations.

Focus point

Physical comedy comes from two sources: the comedian him- or herself and the comedian's interaction with the world.

Obviously it helps if the performer looks funny in some way, but more often than not this is an illusion created by posture, facial expression and clothes. Look at Rowan Atkinson as Mr Bean and as Blackadder and you'll see how this works.

Interactions with the world can be with other people, animals or objects. One of the key types of interaction involves violence. For some reason, we love to laugh at the most extreme sufferings of other people, and physical comedians can expect to be assaulted in endless ways.

Another important type of interaction involves helpless clumsiness. The rest of the world, whether animate or inanimate, is an puzzle that can never be solved – taps won't turn on then suddenly gush water, gates won't open, chairs collapse and technology never works.

Mime is a highly specialized form of visual performance, which can be not only funny but also moving, serious and profound. Mime artists traditionally use white face paint and tight black clothing and are often street performers. However, a more modern take on mime is possible. Rowan Atkinson playing an invisible drum kit or piano is not strictly mime as there is a sound accompaniment, but it is very funny.

Take an everyday object...

Take an everyday object and see how many funny things you can do with it, both clumsy and violent.

Count Arthur Strong, via Steve Delaney

'A common mistake new comedy writers make is trying not to make mistakes. Making mistakes is good. Don't worry about it. It's a fine way of learning.'

Incongruity

Make a list of at least ten incongruous things. Don't try to be funny, and be as random as possible. Examples of incongruity are an elegant woman whose lipstick is smudged, a baby holding a gun, and a swear word in the middle of a love poem.

Examine your incongruities

Take your list of incongruous things and decide whether each one is funny in itself or could be funny in the right circumstances. Can you think of any incongruities that can just never be funny?

Where to next?

OK, now the basics are in place, let's take a look at the comedy writing mindset and the three factors that create comedy: the audience, the medium and the material.

2

The comedy writing mindset

There is a big difference between enjoying comedy and being able to write comedy. Sounds obvious, but just think about it a moment. Plenty of people who love food are hopeless cooks themselves. Most spectators at the Cup Final are not great footballers. And how many rock music lovers never get further than playing air guitar?

Any kind of writing is hard work, and the rewards are uncertain. If you're buying into a dream of fame and fortune, then look for an easier route. On the other hand, if you struggled in English lessons at school, don't let that stop you. Writing comedy is not about passing exams or being top of the class. It's about making people laugh, and for that you'll need a comedy writing mindset.

In this chapter you will learn about the three essential elements of comedy and how to get into the comedy mindset.

Rob Grant, love lord, writer, producer and *Red Dwarf* co-creator

'A common mistake new comedy writers make is thinking that things that are funny in real life are going to be equally funny in a script, without any adjustments. Just because something actually happened doesn't mean it's believable. When football commentators say, "You couldn't write this", what they really mean is, "If you wrote this, everyone would think it was contrived and incredible and really, really bad writing."'

The elements of comedy

Comedy is created by three factors: the audience, the medium and the material. You can think of this as a triangle, because the three are inextricably linked, and the top point of the triangle belongs to the audience. Without it, there is no comedy.

Write about a comedy you like

Choose a popular comedy that you like very much – a movie, a book or a sitcom. Write a description of the following:

1   Each of the main characters
2   The situation that the characters are in
3   The basics of the plot – for a sitcom choose one favourite episode
4   The style of writing
5   The style of acting (for a movie or a sitcom).

Collect jokes

Collect 20 jokes. Work out why they're funny.

1 THE AUDIENCE

Initially, you'll write for yourself. Everybody does this to start with, but if you are the only person who finds your work funny then you won't have much of a future as a comedy writer. It is only when you begin to write for an audience that you'll have started the journey from amateur to professional.

Defining your audience

'The audience' is whoever is on the receiving end of your work. It might be hundreds of people watching a live performance or one person alone in their bedroom reading your novel. Whoever they are, you'll need to reach them and have respect for them. That doesn't mean buttering them up, but it does mean making them laugh.

Initially, your audience will almost certainly be people like you. If you're an angst-ridden teenage boy or a harassed mother, you'll find it easiest to reach out to people in the same situation as you. You know how they feel, you know what they're going through, and you and they will instinctively understand the humour of the situation. When Spike Milligan wrote *The Goon Show*, he drew on his experience in the army during the Second World War. All comedy is specific in this way.

At the same time, you'll find there is a universal element. If you write about being young, older people in your audience will use their own memories to connect with your comedy. If you write about being old, young people in your audience will think about older people they know. When *The Goon Show* was first broadcast during the 1950s, the entire nation knew something of military life and could connect with it.

Focus point

Basically you'll have a core audience of people like you, who will immediately connect with your humour, and a wider audience of people who can still connect with your humour in some way, at some level.

Reaching your audience

How do you reach your audience? There are some direct routes – such as open-mic nights (if you're willing to perform), blogs and self-published novels – but on the whole you'll find that you have to go via someone else. This could be a book publisher, a magazine editor, a radio producer, a commissioning editor at a TV production company or a theatre script reader. All of these people stand between you and your audience, and it can be quite annoying to find that you have to persuade them to take you on before you can even think about reaching your actual target.

All I can say is, get over it – that's how it is. These people have power, but they also have responsibility. Some of them have mega-bucks to spend, and they all have their jobs on the line if they mess up. Almost all of them are looking for the Next Big Thing, although some may be after a quirkier take that will only ever find a niche audience.

So start by writing what you want to write, what amuses you and what you'd like to see, read or hear. Then learn how to modify and improve it to reach a bigger audience. That is the heart of the difference between amateur and professional.

Focus point

Amateurs sit back when they've finished writing, amazed and delighted with themselves and fully expecting the world to beat a pathway to their door. Professionals are equally amazed and delighted, but have learned not to have those expectations. After a short break, they set about polishing and rewriting until the work is ready for public exposure.

Write about a comedy you don't like

Choose a popular comedy that you dislike – a movie, a book or a sitcom. Write a description of the following:
1   Each of the main characters
2   The situation that the characters are in
3   The basics of the plot – for a sitcom choose one episode
4   The style of writing
5   The style of acting (for a movie or a sitcom).

2 THE MEDIUM

Do you want to write for performance or publication? TV or theatre? Books or journalism? No doubt you already know which medium you're drawn to, and while there is some crossover there are also important differences. Jokes that work on the page are nothing on the screen, and vice versa.

The experience of being a writer differs between media as well. Journalists are on much shorter deadlines than novelists. All forms of performance are team efforts, and you'll need to be able to accept input from other people. The performer is the means by which the material is delivered to the audience so in that sense the performer is the medium, and you'll have to take that into account.

3 THE MATERIAL

This is the point of the triangle that belongs to you, the comedy writer. It's what this book is about. Let's start with the basics.

Watch TV

Watch a recorded episode of any sitcom. Write out what happens in each scene and try to work out what makes it funny.

Lesley Bown, writer

'I was at a university drinks do, chatting and laughing with a group of people who included David Lodge, the novelist and playwright. Suddenly he said to one of us, "Now, that's funny – you don't mind if I use it, do you?" A comedy writer is never off duty.'

Notebook

This simple low-tech device will soon become your best friend. Have one that's small enough to slip into a pocket, along with a pencil (almost anything else is likely to leak into your pocket). If you're a techno-geek you might like an electronic gizmo, but on the whole pencil and paper are easier and cheaper. And then use your notebook to – yes, that's right – make notes. Don't rely on your memory: when you see or hear something amusing, or an idea pops into your head out of the blue, get it written down pronto.

There is a drawback to the notebook concept, which is that if you find that ideas tend to flow when you're driving you obviously can't write anything down. Even groping for a little recording device is not recommended. I've never found a solution to that one.

Time

Because notebooks are easy to lose, you need to make time to transcribe your notes across to your laptop or PC regularly. Making time for transcribing your notes is only the start of it. You will need time to write, time to rewrite, time to network, time to send material out and so on. If you really want to get your comedy out there, you'll need to be organized as well as creative and you'll need to find time for both aspects of the work. But rather than worry about this, approach it from the other direction. Decide how much time you have available and work with that.

Look at your life and decide where you can make time for writing. However busy you are, you should be able to juggle your timetable. Maybe you can cut down the time you spend watching TV, get up earlier, or stay up later. If you're a commuter, can you write on the train? If you're a parent, how about the time you spend waiting while your kids are at an activity?

 Key idea

It's a good idea to formally set time aside for writing. Waiting until you have a free moment, or having vague ideas about when you'll write, is very unlikely to be productive.

Friends in high places

It's easy enough, after a few rejections, to feel you're bashing your head against a locked and bolted door that will never open. Looking at other, more successful writers, you may start to wonder whether they were somebody's relative, or went to school with somebody, or had some other way in that was unfair. There's no point in getting bogged down with this one. Having friends in high places will quite possibly unlock that door and open it a crack, but that's all. Once through the door, you still have deliver the comedy, and the audience still has to like it.

In any case, you can find your own way through. It's called networking. Get out there and meet people – starting with your local comedy scene.

 Focus point

Build up relationships, establish a reputation for being funny, hardworking and reliable, and sooner or later the door will start to swing open.

Working with other people

There's a long tradition of comedy writers working in pairs: Muir and Norden, Galton and Simpson, Dick Clement and Ian La Frenais, French and Saunders. Even the five Pythons worked as two writing pairs and a singleton. It works really well if you each have different talents, but it's not so good if you have the same strengths and weaknesses.

For a writing partnership to be successful, you have to have a level of trust in each other, so that each one feels free to say anything, however lame and unfunny it turns out to be. If you're worried about getting a sarcastic putdown from the other person, then you'll seize up and find it hard to let the ideas flow. It also doesn't help if you get competitive with each other, and you'll need a way of dealing with arguments. I've worked with three different writers and we made copious use of email, but it soon became apparent that it was best for only one person to work on a piece at a time, because otherwise we ended up with multiple versions.

Key idea

Comedy seems to lend itself to writing in pairs because you can test the material on each other and know straight away whether it will get a laugh.

Analysing comedy

Return to the comedy that you like very much. Look at each aspect of it in turn and say what it is that you like about it.

- Is it one or more of the characters?
- Is it the situation?
- Is it the plot or some aspect of the plot?
- Is it the style of writing?
- Is it one or more of the performances (for a movie or sitcom)?

Now return to the comedy that you dislike. Look at each aspect of it in turn and say what it is that you dislike about it.

- Is it one or more of the characters?
- Is it the situation?
- Is it the plot or some aspect of the plot?
- Is it the style of writing?
- Is it one or more of the performances (for a movie or sitcom)?

 ## Robert Ross, comedy historian and writer

'One mistake new comedy writers often make is to second-guess what people want. Don't write like your peers and don't write for a broad, international audience. The chances are that if your partner laughs, more than enough people will also see the joke.'

Comedy mindset dos and don'ts

'Dos and don'ts' may sound like a whole set of rules but, as with everything in this book, think of it more as a series of guidelines. If you can ignore the list and still be successful, that's fine, but for most writers, especially when they first start out, working within the guidelines is the best way forward.

☑ **Don't try to be funny**, at least not when you first start work. Write down everything you think of, whether it's funny, tragic or just plain boring. If you limit yourself to only looking for funny ideas, you'll dam up your creative juices.

☑ **Do keep everything you write.** When things aren't going well, frustration can make you screw up the paper and throw it in the bin, or delete the file. Don't do that – you just never know what might be useful later on. Build up a joke collection for future reference.

☑ **Do stay up to date with popular culture.** As soon as a new gadget appears on the market, a new TV programme becomes popular, or a new catchphrase does the rounds, there will be new opportunities for jokes.

- ☑ **Do have an opinion on everything.** There isn't much comedy in the balanced viewpoint.
- ☑ **Do be a comedy consumer.** Watch sitcoms, go to open-mic nights, see comedy at the theatre, read funny books, and look at the cartoons in newspapers and magazines. Don't confine yourself to your favourites – have a look at everything.
- ☑ **Do keep going till it's really funny.** Many comedy writers say they don't get anything really funny till around the seventh attempt. The outstanding writers don't stop there – they keep going. The harder you push yourself, the funnier it gets.
- ☑ **Do read your work out loud.** Whether it's a novel or a sitcom, you need to listen to the rhythms of your writing.
- ☑ **Do be prepared to work hard.** No one ever said it was going to be easy.

Superheroes!

Play the superheroes game. Invent superheroes with bizarre supernatural gifts and work out how they would save the planet. For instance, your superhero might have the power to turn sprouts into chocolates or the power to make all estate agents tell the truth.

Jan Etherington, award-winning comedy writer, broadcaster and journalist

'Read it aloud! That way, you discover whether your dialogue is real or whether you are writing "sitcom" speak. You'll hear the rhythm of your characters' voices and learn to recognize – and banish – "Harry The Explainer", i.e. clunky exposition: "Brian is your brother. He may be younger than you and still a student but he can't help it if Sylvia finds him attractive, even though she was once engaged to you."'

Workshop

You've now looked in detail at two comedies, one you like and one you dislike, and you've analysed what it is about each of them that drives your preferences. Now try to understand why the two comedies were popular. Inevitably this will feel harder for the comedy you dislike, but try to be objective for both of them.

- Was there something that appealed to a particular audience?
- Was it building on a previous success?
- Did it capture the mood of the moment?
- Was it instantly popular or more of a slow burn?
- How important was the writing to the success of the comedy in question?

Where to next?

How are you going to get started with writing comedy? As with all writing, it starts with ideas.

3

Getting started

Whatever type of comedy you plan to write, you'll need to generate funny ideas, write them out, and polish them. In the course of doing this you'll create a great deal of material that won't be relevant to your current project. Keep it. Keep everything. If you start to be successful as a writer, you'll have a ready-made fund of material to draw on.

You'll soon devise your own way of working. Some writers like to plan everything in detail; others like to plunge in and see where the writing takes them. You certainly don't have to start at the beginning and work through to the end. In fact, it's best to draft out anything that is nagging at you so that you clear your head.

In this chapter you'll learn about using the mixture of anarchy and discipline that is the essence of comedy, and where to look for ideas.

Candy Guard, comic artist (*Pond Life*, *The Observer*)

'If I had to give just one piece of comedy writing advice it would be: train your brain to observe your own responses to everything and anything, however painful or ridiculous. Then be brutally honest. That means learning to laugh at yourself, the hardest lesson of all. Take the funniest bits, test them on a few friends and package them up neatly. Then be generous and admit them to your audience, encouraging them to have the same liberating experience, yet with a comforting sense of "Thank God! It's not just me!"'

The basic stages of writing are:

1 Generate ideas.
2 Write a draft.
3 Rewrite and polish.

All three require you to be both creative and hardworking. You'll need that exhilarating mix of anarchy and discipline that all artists use in their work.

Focus point

Don't spend time polishing your work until after you've finished a complete draft, because you're bound to have to cut some stuff.

A useless inheritance

Someone has died and left you an item of great sentimental value but of no real use to you. Think of all the things you could do with the object, including physical impossibilities that could only happen in the world of the cartoon. For example, take a flowery china teapot. If you blew down the spout, would you get bubbles or music? Would you make tea in it or use it as a urinal?

Anarchy

All comedy is anarchic in that it undermines the status quo and allows people to get away with outrageous behaviour that breaks all the social rules. This is why comedy can be used with serious intent and to make political points, although often, of course, the anarchy is only there to create laughter. Whether it is Wee Jimmy Krankie getting laughs out of mischief that would never be tolerated in a real child, or Malcolm Tucker showing the dark side of politics in *The Thick Of It*, there is always an element of anarchy.

Part of your task as a comedy writer is to unleash your inner anarchist. Let down all the barriers: forget about taste, political correctness and the conventions of society. Think the unthinkable, say the unsayable. Doing this is enormously liberating, but remember that it is just a writing exercise: I'm not suggesting you should try walking naked down your local high street, although you'd certainly acquire plenty of comedy material if you did.

Another way of looking at the anarchic side of comedy is to think of it as playtime. Revert to childhood, forget your worries and just have fun. Let go of your social conditioning and be as rude, silly and disrespectful as you like.

Use some writing sessions to generate ideas, allowing your mind to be as wild and free as possible. The only rule of these sessions is to record everything, either by writing it down or by using a voice recorder.

Before you start, take a moment to clear your mind of your everyday concerns – family worries, unpaid bills and so on. Even let go of your desires for this particular piece of writing. Forget about deadlines, who you're writing for (or would like to write for) and your acceptance speech when you win an award. All of these concerns will cramp you into a mental box and stop you going to the limits of possibility.

The forehead game

One way to get in touch with your inner anarchist is by playing silly games with other people. For instance, try the forehead game. Everyone writes the name of someone famous on a sticky note and the notes are stuck to people's foreheads without them seeing the name. Each person takes turns to guess the name on their own forehead. They can ask any question but the other players can answer only yes or no. If the answer is no, the game moves on to the next person. If the answer is yes, the person can ask another question. Keep going till everyone knows the name on their forehead.

Miranda Hart, comedy actress and writer

'If I had to give just one piece of comedy writing advice, it would be to write what you think is funny: don't try to appeal to a certain demographic or do what you think the broadcasters might like.'

GENERATING MATERIAL

You've shut yourself away with pencil and paper and promised yourself a good dose of anarchy and playtime to get the ideas flowing. What if nothing happens? You'll feel self-conscious and awkward and not at all funny. Here are a few suggestions to kick-start the process. When you're trying any of these, don't pay any attention to the quality of the ideas. That comes later. All you need to do at first is allow ideas to emerge. Most of them will be rubbish and many of them will be embarrassingly bad, but it is important never to worry about your rubbish ideas and unfunny jokes at this stage – just be prepared to remove them during the editing process.

Freethinking

The classic way to freethink is to use a big piece of paper. Write your central topic in the middle and draw a circle round it, with lines radiating out. At the end of the lines, write ideas connected with the topic, draw circles round them and lines radiating out, then add more connected words and so on. Don't restrict yourself or strain to be original you can be both conventional and wacky since both might lead to something useful. In fact, don't censor anything. That comes later in a discipline session.

Lists

No, not the dreaded 'to-do' list. Lists of almost anything can be used to generate ideas and are the comedy writer's great standby. Rather like freethinking, you can make a list of words associated with a single topic or take one word and see how many different topics it can be associated with. We'll look at this in greater detail in other chapters.

A shopping list

Here's a random shopping list:

Onions

Toothbrush

Wrapping paper

Paper clips

Frying pan

Write a short paragraph that features all of them, but don't mention shopping.

Rob Grant, love lord, writer, producer and *Red Dwarf* co-creator

'*Study other comedy writers. Select writers whose work you admire, find anything you can that they might have written or said in interviews about comedy writing, and deconstruct their work to try to figure out how they did it. Obviously, you shouldn't be copying them, but you'll be surprised what you can work out about technique and craft from them.*'

Discipline

Anarchy is only one side of the coin. All writing requires discipline once the initial wave of inspiration and enthusiasm has swept past. If you are writing for someone else, you will need to meet their deadlines – the last thing you want is a reputation for being unreliable. Even if you're writing for yourself, you will need to keep on producing material, because the more you exercise your writing muscles the stronger and more flexible they become.

This is also the time to put back some of the taste, social conventions and political correctness that you so gaily abandoned in the anarchy sessions. This is a matter of individual judgement and how you see yourself as a comedy writer. Do you want to shock, entertain or educate? It's up to you.

As you look through your material, think of yourself as a miner in the Gold Rush, panning through the dirt and silt to find the tiny nuggets of gold. One difficulty is that you won't be able to use them all. You'll always have some wonderfully funny material that just isn't right for the piece you're working on. Just like gold, it will keep its value, so add it to your comedy file.

Focus point

If you find yourself struggling to resolve problems in your writing, revert to an anarchy session to help you think outside the box.

In comedy writing, every word has to be there for a reason, and almost always the best way to get to the laugh is also the quickest. If you want to delay the laugh for some reason, then you have to give your audience something along the way – a smaller laugh, or something that keeps their interest.

Whether you're writing a one-liner or a novel, you need to know how it's going to end. You may not know this when you first start writing, but at some point you'll realize where you're going.

Key idea

Once you know what the ending is going to be, you'll need to revise everything you've written so far to make sure it relates to the ending in some way.

Rewrite a fairy tale

Here's a brief summary of the story of Little Red Riding Hood:

'Little Red Riding Hood is told to take her Granny some cake because she's ill in bed.

Walking through the woods, Little Red Riding Hood meets a wolf, who persuades her to leave the path and pick some flowers. The wolf runs ahead to Granny's cottage and swallows Granny whole. Then he puts on Granny's cap and nightgown and climbs into her bed. When Little Red Riding Hood arrives at the cottage, she notices that Granny seems to have a big nose, big eyes and very big teeth. She realizes that something is wrong, so she shouts for help just as the wolf is about to eat her. A woodcutter arrives to save her, splits the wolf open with his axe and out jumps Granny, quite unhurt.'

Work out how you would tell the story:

- from the point of view of Granny
- from the point of view of the Wolf.

Sources of comedy ideas

Comedy doesn't just appear from nowhere, and most of the time it's no good waiting for inspiration to strike. If you want to write comedy, you have to go out and get some ideas. Luckily, they're all around you.

PEOPLE

Comedy is about people, and people are everywhere. Just keep your eyes and ears open and you'll soon start to gather material. Learn to sit quietly in public places and watch what is going on. Sometimes you can't help overhearing, too.

People watching

Next time you're out and about, spend some time people watching. Just sit quietly and let the comedy come to you.

Lesley Bown, writer

'I used to hate queuing, until I realized that just by standing there and doing nothing I could be collecting comedy material. Now I love to queue.'

DAYDREAMS

Some would say that this is the best bit of being writer. Lie back, close your eyes, and let your thoughts drift. If you combine this with a hot bath, you can't be accused of time wasting.

EMOTIONS

A lot of comedy writing is driven by negative emotions. When you experience anger and frustration, look for the comedy in what has happened. For instance, there was a time when most stand-up routines seemed to include a rant about being put on hold or about the menus on phone helplines. The frustrations of everyday life are great material, and so, too, are the bigger issues that arouse our anger.

 ## What makes you angry?

Make a list of things that make you angry, and give your reasons. These are your comedy targets.

If you're going to use comedy as a vent for your emotions, you need to be aware of certain boundaries. If the target of your comedy is in the audience, then make your jokes only about things that aren't important to them personally. Think of a typical best man's speech at a wedding, which may be full of digs at the bridegroom but would go badly wrong if it revealed unpleasant truths. Even if you feel justified in the attack, the effect will only be to make the audience uncomfortable and turn them against you and your message.

Of course, in most comedy situations the target isn't present, but there are still good and bad ways of venting emotion. Some targets are fair game, (politicians, the royal family) and what they generally have in common is that they're perceived to be above the comedian and the audience in the social hierarchy. Generally, when we find comedy objectionable, it's because it's aiming downwards rather than upwards.

Key idea

Undermining authority figures is acceptable; attacking the disadvantaged just isn't.

Edit your anger list

Examine your list of things that make you angry and divide them into categories. For instance, they might be:

- personal (e.g. the way there's never enough hot water left for your morning shower)
- political (e.g. the effect of government financial cuts on your local community)
- global (e.g. the destruction of the rainforests).

FACE TIME

Getting together with other people can be a good way of generating ideas. You can socialize with your mates in a casual way or deliberately meet up with your comedy contacts to work on ideas. Expect a high wastage rate, though. You'll find that many jokes that seemed hysterically funny at the pub after a couple of beers turn out not to have any legs at all. Remember that private jokes among friends are always more extreme than public ones, and edit accordingly.

FRIENDS AND FAMILY

Most of us find this one all too easy. Every family has a story to tell and most of these have comedy potential. However, how they will feel about you telling their story is quite another matter and outside the remit of this book.

THE MEDIA

Here is another big advantage of being a comedy writer. You really do need to watch a lot of TV, go to the theatre and cinema, and read newspapers and magazines. You're not idling – you're doing research. You can home in on current affairs, celebrities or any other aspect of our culture.

OLD STORIES

Think of this as roughly everything that is out of copyright but still within general cultural awareness, for example *Alice in Wonderland* or *Robinson Crusoe*. (Copyright in the UK lasts for an author's lifetime and for 70 years after their death.) It also includes myths, folk tales and fairy stories. With all of these you can retell the story with a modern twist, in the way that *West Side Story* was a retelling of *Romeo and Juliet* – of course, you'll be looking to make it funny. Another very useful comedy technique is to retell a story from the point of view of a minor character. For instance, in 1983 Keith Waterhouse rewrote *The Diary of a Nobody* (1892) from the point of view of the wife – he called it *Mrs Pooter's Diary*.

It's important to choose old stories that you can expect your audience to be familiar with. Most of us know about *Red Riding Hood*; very few of us know *The Saga of Erik the Red*.

Workshop

Look again at the list of things that make you angry. For each one, decide how you would use comedy to vent your anger. Ask yourself:

- How can I create recognition?
- How can I create surprise?
- How can I persuade people to share my anger?
- How can keep the audience on my side?

Where to next?

Language is very important to almost all comedy, so the next chapter takes a brief look at that, with further information in Appendix D.

4

Language and style

Comedy writing is all about words. You may be seeing hysterically funny pictures in your head, but unless you can put them into words no one will ever know. The language you choose to use – both vocabulary and grammar – will affect both the style and the content of your work and it will vary according to whether you are writing for performance or for reading.

In this chapter you will learn about working with words and developing your style, using the rhythms of language (pauses, sentence structure and grammar) and creating word pictures in the minds of your audience.

In many areas of life, we're inclined to be rather dismissive of style ('all style and no substance') but in writing, style is absolutely crucial. You can write:

> Dear Sir or Madam, It has come to my attention that you are in arrears...

or you can write:

> Hi, I just remembered that you owe me some dough.

The content is the same but the style is entirely different. If the style is wrong in some way, then the content simply won't be communicated. Neither of the sentences above is funny in itself, but you might be heading for a laugh if the first one was a note a mother put in her child's sandwiches, and the second one was a letter from a bank manager trying to be customer friendly.

Key idea

In the case of comedy, style is a large part of what makes people laugh.

Count Arthur Strong, via Steve Delaney

'If I had to give just one piece of comedy writing advice it would be to try to be as original as you can. Don't pinch my material. (That's two, but concisely done!)'

Workshop

Read the following extract from *The Diary of a Nobody* by George and Weedon Grossmith and then answer the questions that follow.

'**April 29.**—I am getting quite accustomed to being snubbed by Lupin, and I do not mind being sat upon by Carrie because I think she has a certain amount of right to do so; but I do think it hard to be at once snubbed by wife, son, and both my guests.

'Gowing and Cummings had dropped in during the evening, and I suddenly remembered an extraordinary dream I had a few nights ago, and I thought I would tell them about it. I dreamed I saw some huge blocks of ice in a shop with a bright glare behind them. I walked into the shop and the heat was overpowering. I found that the blocks of ice were on fire. The whole thing was so real and yet so supernatural I woke up in a cold perspiration. Lupin in a most contemptuous manner, said: "What utter rot."

'Before I could reply, Gowing said there was nothing so completely uninteresting as other people's dreams.

'I appealed to Cummings, but he said he was bound to agree with the others and my dream was especially nonsensical. I said: "It seemed so real to me." Gowing replied: "Yes, to *you* perhaps, but not to *us*." Whereupon they all roared.

'Carrie, who had hitherto been quiet, said: "He tells me his stupid dreams every morning nearly." I replied: "Very well, dear, I promise you I will never tell you or anybody else another dream of mine the longest day I live." Lupin said: "Hear! hear!" and helped himself to another glass of beer. The subject was fortunately changed, and Cummings read a most interesting article on the superiority of the bicycle to the horse.'

- What sort of man is the author of this diary? Make a list of the qualities you detect in him from the way he writes his diary.
- Does this extract make you want to read more? If not, why not?
- In your opinion, does the extract work as humour? Say why, or why not.
- *The Diary of a Nobody* was first published in 1892. Has the humour dated at all? How would you go about creating a modern version?

A sense of rhythm

There is a rhythm to all language, and comedy has its own rhythm or, rather, rhythms. Some writers have a natural feel for this, but others have to learn it. It's difficult to teach someone a feeling for rhythm, but you can learn it by absorbing comedy writing and then imitating. Out of this process you'll eventually develop your own rhythm.

Focus point

Reading your work out loud will give you a feel for its rhythm.

Here's an American joke:

> A man dreamed he was a muffler on a car, and then he turned into part of a wheel. He woke up exhausted and tired.

The rhythm of this feels all wrong to me, because we'd normally say 'tired and exhausted'. So I'd want to rewrite the joke:

> A man dreamed he was part of a car wheel, and then he turned into a muffler. He woke up tired and exhausted.

You'll also need to be sensitive to the type of language used by your audience. The American joke doesn't work for the UK since we don't use the word 'muffler'. So here it is rewritten for the UK:

> A man dreamed he was part of a car wheel, and then he turned into an exhaust. He woke up tired and exhausted.

And there's the joke ruined, because the word 'exhaust' in the first sentence anticipates the punchline and gives it away. This joke doesn't travel.

Rhythm in performance can be quite different from rhythm on the page. Most performers have their own way of pacing a joke and audiences learn to tell when the punchline is due. A pause just before it is the most common way:

> I do like children *(pause)* but I couldn't eat a whole one.

The pause makes it obvious that the punchline is next, but there are different rhythms to an afterthought (which comes after the punchline). It can be added quickly, before the audience expects it, or after a longer pause when they should have assumed that the joke was finished and the next one was on its way:

> I do like children *(pause)* but I couldn't eat a whole one.
> *(long pause)* It's different if they're chocolate coated, obviously.

 Key idea

On the page the writer creates rhythm through sentence structure and punctuation.

Although people vary, mostly we don't read one word at a time and we are vaguely aware, as we read, of the next few words ahead of us. If you simply substitute a comma for the pause, the reader will get to the punchline almost before they realize it. This is fine for a joke book, but in continuous prose (novels or journalism) you might want to pace the laugh with a few extra words:

I do like children, truly I do, it's just that I couldn't eat a whole one.

You can add afterthoughts or play with the joke:

He had an expression on his face like someone who, after trotting out his favourite joke that he liked children but couldn't eat a whole one, finds himself offered a plate of tiny chocolate-coated body parts.

Miranda Hart, comedy actress and writer

'Watch, read, learn and absorb from comedy new and old, but don't lose your distinctive voice.'

Practise the rhythm of jokes

Here are the bare bones of five short jokes:

- A boomerang that doesn't come back is a stick.
- A dentist earns his living off bad teeth but also recommends toothpaste.
- If you get crushed under a pile of books you've only got your shelf to blame.
- A lifeguard can't rescue a hippy if he's too far out, man.
- If you eat yeast and shoe polish you'll be able to rise and shine.

Rewrite each one so that it has a good rhythm for:

1 telling
2 reading.

Word pictures

One of the basic tenets of writing is 'Show, don't tell'. With descriptive writing, this means don't simply state the facts. Don't say 'He had an odd-shaped head' because that won't make anyone laugh – there's no funny picture. Instead, look for an image – maybe say, 'He had a head shaped like a rugby ball.' This creates a picture in the minds of your audience, which you can embellish as much as you like: 'He had a head shaped like a rugby ball after an All-Blacks game – a bit battered and with the stitching coming loose.'

Dickens is the past master of this type of description. Since he was paid by the word, he wasn't interested in economy but even so he could sum up a character's appearance in a few words. Here is Mrs Pipchin in *Dombey & Son*:

> 'This celebrated Mrs Pipchin was a marvellous ill-favoured, ill-conditioned old lady, of a stooping figure, with a mottled face, like bad marble, a hook nose, and a hard grey eye, that looked as if it might have been hammered at on an anvil without sustaining any injury.'

Of course, the anvil is not only amusing: it conveys her personality as well. And note that the description builds towards the end, which is both the funniest and the most important part.

Dickens can also do this without using imagery, as in this description of Mr Murdstone's sister in *David Copperfield*:

> A gloomy-looking lady she was; dark, like her brother, whom she greatly resembled in face and voice; and with very heavy eyebrows, nearly meeting over her large nose, as if, being disabled by the wrongs of her sex from wearing whiskers, she had carried them to that account.

Comic description

Describe someone's appearance briefly and in a comedic way. You can use yourself, someone you know, a celebrity or a fictional character.

Adjectives and adverbs

These descriptive words are a two-edged weapon for any writer. Too many of them and your writing will lack focus, too few and it will read like a report.

Focus point

One common piece of advice given to writers is to remove all the adverbs and adjectives from an early draft, and replace only the ones that are absolutely essential. Of course, doing this will have a profound effect on the rhythm of your piece, so read it out loud before you make the final decision.

Dickens, with his financial need for a high word count, tended to sprinkle descriptive words about liberally. It's interesting to look at the two descriptions with most of them taken out:

> This Mrs Pipchin was an old lady, with a face like marble, a hook nose, and a grey eye, that looked as if it might have been hammered at on an anvil without sustaining any injury.'

> She was like her brother, whom she resembled in face and voice; and with eyebrows nearly meeting over her nose, as if, being disabled by the wrongs of her sex from wearing whiskers, she had carried them to that account.

Which do you prefer? For me, Mrs Pipchin reads better without her modifiers and Miss Murdstone is happier with them.

Lists

We've already seen how the rule of three works. You can also use longer lists for comic effect. Here's Jane Austen listing characteristics in a letter to her sister in 1800 – and note the rhythm of the second sentence:

> Mrs Blount was the only one much admired. She appeared exactly as she did in September, with the same broad face, diamond bandeau, white shoes, pink husband, and fat neck.

P.G. Wodehouse created a much longer list to describe someone overdoing the solicitude in *Lord Emsworth Acts for the Best*, with the funniest item at the end (and, incidentally, 'muffler' used in the English sense):

> But when the fellow did the same thing day after day, night after night, every time he caught him sitting; when he offered him an arm to help him across floors; when he assisted him up stairs, along corridors, down paths, out of rooms and into raincoats; when he snatched objects from his hands to carry them himself; when he came galloping out of the house on dewy evenings laden down with rugs, mufflers, hats and, on one occasion, positively, a blasted respirator... why, then Lord Emsworth's proud spirit rebelled.

Using lists

Use a list to describe someone. You can use yourself, someone you know, a celebrity or a fictional character.

Idioms

Idioms are ways of using language that are not literally true but which everyone understands, such as 'rule of thumb' meaning 'rough estimate'. Sometimes an alien with a dictionary could just about work out the meaning of a phrase such as 'get over it', but the most useful idioms to the comedy writer are the ones with no literal connection to the meaning they convey, such as 'fine kettle of fish' meaning 'a mess or a muddle'. Other idioms are subtler, for instance 'don't start anything' means 'don't start trouble'.

You can get laughs from playing around with idioms:

Some jump leads went into a bar and asked for beer.
The barman said, "All right, but just don't start anything."

And here's a Wodehouse example from *The Inimitable Jeeves*:

Warm-hearted! I should think he has to wear asbestos vests...

Alternatively, you can turn idioms upside down: 'pure as the driven snow' can become 'pure as the driven slush.' This works best if the idiom is also a cliché (see below).

 ## Creating laughs from idioms

Here's a list of idioms. What can you do with each one to create a laugh?

- They get on like a house on fire.
- His bark is worse than his bite.
- She bent over backwards to help me.
- It's a whole new ballpark.
- I'm generous to a fault.
- They were all dressed up like a dog's dinner.
- I don't like to be a wet blanket but...
- They made a real hash of it.
- That's not to be sneezed at.
- We decided to go Dutch.

Clichés, aphorisms and proverbs

Clichés, aphorisms and proverbs can be used in similar ways to idioms. Oscar Wilde took 'Nothing succeeds like success' and turned it into the witty 'Nothing succeeds like excess' – unlike the very silly version 'Nothing succeeds (sucks seeds) like a parrot with no teeth.'

You'll have more chances to practise this kind of joke writing in Chapter 5.

Catchphrases

A catchphrase is a phrase repeated so often that it becomes associated with that performer or show. Catchphrases have been documented to as far back as the sixteenth century and they no doubt go back further than that. They're not usually funny as such, but become so through repetition. Stand-up comedians often have a catchphrase and *The Fast Show* allocated a catchphrase to almost every series of sketches.

Key idea

A catchphrase may not be funny in itself: in a vote on the most popular TV catchphrases, Victor Meldrew's 'I don't believe it' was the winner – but this is only funny in context.

Using the wrong language

Write a brief note to a teacher explaining why a child missed a day at school. Now rewrite it using inappropriate language. How many different ways can you think of to do this?

Family stories

Every family has its funny stories, usually about things that at the time were embarrassing or disastrous – the day Granddad's false teeth fell in the punch, the holiday we spent at the airport because of the weather, and so on.

> Write out one of your family stories twice. First, tell it just as it happened; then write about it a second time, embellishing it and changing the facts it to make it funnier. Read both accounts out loud and decide which one you prefer.

Accents and regional speech

There's a lot of comedy value in accents, but you need to know what you're doing. It's best to stick with accents that you know well and can hear in your head as you write. If you're writing for a specific performer, you'll know what they can and can't manage, but if you're writing a script without knowing who will perform it, then only specify an accent if it's absolutely essential.

 ## Focus point

You don't want your script rejected on the grounds that it's too difficult to cast, so think carefully about using accents.

Most accents are part of a larger regional speech, which has a particular rhythm, grammar and vocabulary associated with it. A Cockney character might say, 'Me ol' woman give us a right ear-bashing' and you clearly should not write that as 'My wife gave me quite a telling off.' Some slang words are so well known that you can assume that readers and performers will recognize them, so you can use them rather than the correct form: 'innit' for 'isn't it' is a good example.

Representing accents on the page is a minefield. In a script it's best to mention the accent required at the beginning and then spell the words normally. For example, for a Cockney character you would specify Cockney in the character notes and write 'My old woman give us a right ear-bashing.' This retains the vocabulary and grammatical peculiarities while still being perfectly readable.

 ## Robert Ross, comedy historian and writer

'If I had to give just one piece of comedy writing advice it would be … never give up! You will be hungry, you will be depressed, you will be rejected. One day, you will use all of that to make 'em laugh.'

It's slightly more problematic for prose writers, who need to give a flavour of the accent for every speech without cluttering up the page with punctuation and semi-phonetic spellings. Arnold Bennett got it about right in *The Card*:

> 'Ye're here for th' better part o' some time, then' observed Mrs Hullins, looking facts in the face. 'I've told you about my son Jack. He's been playing six weeks. He starts to-day, and he'll gi'me summat Saturday.'

Whatever you do, avoid the knots D.H. Lawrence managed to tie himself into. Stuff like this from *Lady Chatterley's Lover* is beyond parody:

> 'Why,' he began, in the broad slow dialect. 'Your Ladyship's as welcome as Christmas ter th' hut an'th' key an' iverythink as is. On'y this time O' th' year ther's bods ter set, an' Ah've got ter be potterin' abaht a good bit, seein' after 'em, an' a'. Winter time Ah ned 'ardly come nigh th' pleece. But what wi' spring, an' Sir Clifford wantin' ter start th' pheasants... An' your Ladyship'd non want me tinkerin' around an' about when she was 'ere, all the time.'

Working with accents

Take your note to the teacher from the previous snapshot exercise and rewrite it as a speech, in an accent that you feel comfortable with. Decide how to represent it on the page.

Where to next?

In the next chapter you're going to explore the basic building blocks of comedy – jokes.

5

‹ Jokes

Jokes are the most basic unit of comedy and joke writing is
an important skill that exercises your comedy muscles. Many
aspiring comedy writers are rather dismissive of joke writing,
probably because they remember the traditional style of
stand-up that consisted of a series of quick-fire jokes around
a single topic. Eventually this format became rather tired and
observational comedy, which is more about pointing out the
oddities of real life, replaced it. In fact, many observational
routines do include a few jokes.

In this chapter you will learn how to write short jokes – which
at their simplest consist of just a set-up and punchline – and
then how to edit your jokes to improve them. You'll also find
out how to write extended jokes and about using different
well-known joke formats.

Chris Ritchie, creator of the
Innovative Comedy: Writing
& Performance degree at
Southampton Solent University and
editor of *Comedy Studies*

'*The most common mistake new comedy writers make is
writing a sitcom before they know how to write jokes. I get
people applying to the comedy degree I run who tell me they
have written a sitcom and they haven't even done stand-up
(you don't have to, but it sure helps!). You have to start small
with one-liners, then do a monologue, then expand into
sketches. Also, no one is going to buy a sitcom cold like that.
You have to work your way up or else it is waste of labour
(unless you see it as practising writing). Placing work is hard
but there are ways of getting it on somewhere. Try writing spec
scripts as well. Also, writers perform stand-up – people like Rob
Grant, Stephen Merchant and Robin Ince are on the circuit and
approachable. Talk to them. They know what they're on about.*'

 Focus point

The wheel always turns and joke-based stand-up, which never
entirely went away, is staging something of a revival.

Short jokes

The ability to write jokes – short, self-contained nuggets of humour –
is an important skill for the comedy writer. Short jokes can consist of
just a set-up and punchline:

Set-up: A horse went into a bar.

Punchline: The barman said, 'Why the long face?'

The set-up should include all the information you need to
understand the punchline, without giving it away. In the example
above, just the fact that it's a horse is enough information. Because
it's a formulaic joke, the audience will know at once that the
punchline will be something to do with a horse's characteristics, but,
unless they've heard it before, they won't guess what. It's the surprise
of the twisted logic that creates the laugh.

Single jokes can be extended with afterthoughts to form part of a routine:

A white horse went into a bar.

The barman said, 'Why the long face?'

The horse started coughing.

The barman said, 'You need to be in the horspital.'

The horse said, 'Shut up and gimme a brandy.'

The barman said, 'You know, we have a whisky named after you.'

The horse said 'What, Sebastian?'

Single-frame cartoons are usually based around a joke. The drawing is the set-up and the caption is the punchline.

Like any skill, your joke writing will improve with practice, so try to write 20 jokes a day. As you keep working at it, you'll find your standards gradually rising. At first you'll think of only the obvious jokes but, as you already know, persistence pays. After doing a few, say five or six, you'll find yourself trying a bit harder and reaching that bit higher.

Focus point

Don't worry about the quality at this stage. The aim is to produce quantity and edit out the poor jokes later on, before you submit them anywhere.

Eric Chappell, writer

The most common mistake new comedy writers make is the belief that four weak jokes make one good one. They don't. Wait for the good one.

WRITING SHORT JOKES

To get you started, here is a variety of ways to generate jokes.

Adjectives

A simple specific adjective such as 'green' can be used to generate jokes. Start with a list of everything you can think of connected with green. You might get something like this:

Green light, green for go, Green Line bus, green green grass of home, little green men, green card, Greenpeace, green fees, green tea, green with envy, greenhouse, village green, greenhouse gases, climate change, frogs, apples, cabbage and other vegetables, vegetarianism.

There are more, but you get the idea. Now look for simple jokes using your list, for instance:

When I was a teenager I had a terrible weight problem. I didn't just have puppy fat – when we were on holiday, if I sunbathed on the beach, Greenpeace would send a crew to try and refloat me.

What kind of frog is green and dangerous? One with a machine gun.

You can extend this by looking for the opposites Sticking with green, you might get:

Red, stop, pollution, climate change denial, driving an SUV, carnivorism, and so on.

Use the opposites to generate more jokes:

My doctor told me to eat more greens, so last night I had a steak. Cows eat grass, don't they?

 ## Jokes from adjectives

Choose an adjective, make the lists and then see how many jokes you can generate – aim for 20. If you can't manage 20 jokes from one adjective, repeat the process with others.

Everyday items

The everyday items don't have to be funny – in fact, the more mundane the better. Start by researching alternative uses, for instance:

Vodka: use vodka to clean jewellery, polish a chandelier, remove lipstick from clothing, clean greenfly off houseplants.

And then look for the jokes:

I read somewhere you can use vodka to get lipstick off your collar, so I drank half a bottle – I couldn't see the lipstick but my wife could. Next time I'll get her to drink the vodka.

Don't use vodka to clean greenfly off houseplants. They'll just throw a party and invite all the other bugs.

Jokes from everyday items

Make a list of 20 everyday items, things we all use. Now seek out alternative uses for each one and write as many jokes as you can.

Get visual

You don't have to be able to draw to create cartoon humour. You can use pictures from magazines, for instance a photo of two celebrities on the red carpet might be captioned with the shorter person saying 'I can see right up your nose'. You can draw simple things yourself – stick people, flowers, or even geometric shapes. For example, you could draw two identical flowers with the caption 'There's something I really like about you.' Or flowers looking up at a leafy tree with the caption 'He won't be so full of it come the autumn.'

Clichés and proverbs

The more often clichés and proverbs are used the better their potential for humour. The idea is to play with a well-known saying in an unexpected and incongruous way:

> Been there, done that, got the T-shirt, worn it and turned into dusters.

> People who live in glasshouses shouldn't leave the curtains open at bathtime.

You can also undermine a cliché or proverb with an add-on. 'Money can't buy you happiness' could give:

> Money can't buy you happiness, but it makes the kids stay in touch.

Or you can look for a reverse:

> If money can't buy you happiness, then why do we pay for chocolate?

Working with clichés and proverbs

Make a list of 20 clichés or proverbs. See what happens if you:
- take each one to its logical extreme
- turn each one on its head
- assume each one is literally true
- extend each one with an add-on
- reverse each one.

Definitions

There are two ways of getting a joke from a definition. The first way is to play with the meaning of the word and come up with another meaning that reveals a truth:

Experience: the name people give to their mistakes.

The other way is to ignore the correct meaning and find another based on the sound of the word:

Negligent: absentmindedly answering the front door in your nightie.

New definitions

Make a list of 20 abstract nouns (for example: happiness, jealousy, peculiarity) and write alternative definitions for each one.

Oddities

Two items that don't appear to have any connection can be paired to make a joke. Let's say our pair is tennis racquets and toasters:

My toaster shoots the toast into the air. Still, if I catch it with my tennis racquet I get instant croutons.

Odd couples

Take your list of 20 everyday objects and create ten pairs. Create a joke from each pairing.

Professions and hobbies

You can generate lots of jokes from people's work or interests. The light-bulb joke is one of the classic formats:

Q. How many computer programmers does it take to change a light bulb?

A. Only one, but why bother, the light socket will be obsolete in six months anyway.

They can also be used to generate funny names, for instance:

Librarians: Otto Biographie, Allison Wonderland

Sometimes these are funnier presented in two stages:

Mr and Mrs Wallcarpet, and their son, Walter Wallcarpet.

Jokes from professions and hobbies

Make a list of 20 groups of people (by profession or hobby) and write light-bulb jokes for them, then generate funny names.

Read the news

Newspaper headlines will produce jokes with a short shelf life, but there is always a demand for them. The real comedy gold, however, is found in the inside pages and within small news items. Scientists and researchers are particularly fruitful:

Research has shown that a teenager costs thousands of pounds – but why would anybody want to buy one?

Researchers who discovered that the smell of roses and chocolates induces romantic feelings have been unable to account for the popularity of diamond rings.

Workshop

1 Buy a newspaper and use the contents to create 20 jokes.
2 Cut out 20 photos from magazines, the quirkier the better. Write funny captions for each one.
3 Next, move on to creating your own simple visuals. Create 20 cartoons using the same 'characters'.

Insults

There is nothing like a clever insult to get an audience laughing:

My ex believed that money can't buy you happiness, which is why he never spent any money on me.

He has a mind like a steel trap - always closed.

Get personal

Look through all your lists and write 20 insults.

Editing short jokes

Once you've written your first batch of 20 jokes, leave them for a day or so and then start editing them – but remember, don't throw anything away. Even a weak joke might be useful one day as part of a build-up to a bigger laugh, or you might see a way of improving it.

 ## Lesley Bown, writer

'The very first joke I sold was for radio, a spoof news item that was just over 100 words. They rewrote it and broadcast 60 words. I was lucky to sell it, and I never made that mistake again.'

 ## Focus point

When you have edited out your worst jokes, put them in a Bad Jokes folder rather than delete them.

Before you start work, there are a few key things to remember:

1 **Be economical with words.** In a short joke, every word has to earn its keep. For instance, the Greenpeace joke is much improved by being shortened:

> I didn't just have puppy fat; when I sunbathed on the beach Greenpeace would try to refloat me.

2 **Keep the best till last.** Make sure the laugh is on the last word, for instance:

> If money can't buy happiness, then why isn't chocolate free?

3 **Don't reveal the punchline in the set-up** – this is usually a question of avoiding one key word. For instance, removing 'frog' from my earlier set-up gives this:

> What's green and dangerous? A frog with a machine gun.

4 **Use specific vocabulary.** Don't say 'dog', say 'poodle' or 'Doberman' – it helps create a more vivid picture. For instance:

> My ex believed that money can't buy you happiness, which is why I never had an engagement ring.

5 **Don't be too direct.** If you say 'he looked like a vicar' it won't get a laugh, but you might get a small laugh from:

> 'I took one look at him and booked him for my son's christening.'

Edit your jokes

Look through all the jokes you've generated in the previous exercises and edit each one till it is as slick and quick as possible. Then choose which ones are going to go into your Bad Jokes folder.

Extended jokes

Longer jokes are more like a funny short story:

> A farmer was showing a visitor round his farm. When they got to the pigsty, the visitor noticed one of the pigs had a wooden leg. 'Poor thing,' he said to the farmer, 'how did that happen?' 'Ah,' said the farmer, 'that's a very special pig, that is. One night we were all asleep in the farmhouse and a spark from the fire set the house alight. The pig could smell the burning so he jumped out of the sty, ran to the house, broke in through a window, ran upstairs and dragged me out of bed. Then he went back into the burning house and rescued the rest of the family. He even got the dog and the budgie out. Yes siree, that's quite a special pig.' 'Amazing,' said the visitor, 'but how did he get the wooden leg?' 'Oh come on,' said the farmer, 'you can't eat a pig like that all in one go.'

As you can see, there are no laughs along the way in a joke of this sort. It all hangs on the punchline – and it's just as likely to be greeted with a groan as a laugh. This type of joke is for telling to friends rather than for use in a professional context – not many paying audiences will wait that long for a laugh. Ronnie Corbett developed a technique for telling a long joke by using constant asides to raise small laughs before the big one at the end, rather like this:

> A farmer was showing a visitor round his farm. Well, I say farm, it was more like a factory with animals. Not that they minded, though – you should've seen those chickens queuing up to clock in. So anyway, when they got to the pigsty...

A professional comedy writer would also see at once that the joke needs to be more specific:

> My cousin had a mid-life crisis. He left his highly stressful job as an estate agent, I mean you know how difficult it can be measuring rooms, and he bought a farm. So I went to visit him one day...

WRITING A LONG JOKE

This is often about finding an anecdote to fit a punchline, since most of the length of the joke is in the set-up. You can see that the farmer joke above could have taken any number of routes to get to the punchline. Try to construct a route that appears to be leading off in quite a different direction so that the surprise at the end is as big as possible, because the audience has had to wait for it. The route chosen for the farmer joke points the audience at the fire, which distracts them before the punchline.

Avoid using any key words and concepts in the body of the joke. Don't, for instance, do this:

> When they got to the pigsty, the visitor noticed that one of the pigs had a wooden leg. He said, 'What a shame, one less roasting joint off that one'.

Write a long joke

Look through the jokes you've already written, choose one of the punchlines and write a long joke for it. If none of them seems suitable, use this punning punchline: 'What's this left ear/left 'ere?'

SHAGGY DOG STORIES

The idea of a shaggy dog story is to make the joke as long as possible (a four-hour car journey gives the lover of shaggy dogs an ideal opportunity) and in its purest form the shaggy dog has no punchline at all – it just reaches an anti-climax and stops. The classic joke of this form is about a man who buys a dog that is very shaggy, and everyone he speaks to agrees that the dog is the shaggiest they've ever seen (and this list of people can go on for ever) until the very last person says, 'It isn't that shaggy' and the joke ends.

While your friends and family may be extremely tolerant of this type of joke, in a professional situation it's a risky strategy that depends very much on the performer. Another type of shaggy dog, that leads to an unexpected and ridiculous pun, has a better chance of success. Here's a short version, but a seasoned shaggy dog teller would make it much longer than this:

> A man was famous for the wonderful tulips he grew. People used to come from all over just to admire them and to try and get the secret of how he grew them. No one could discover just what it was that turned ordinary bulbs into the most beautiful tulips. One day his friend decided that he would get the secret out of

him. He went round one evening with a few bottles of wine and as the tulip grower got drunker and drunker the friend gradually turned the conversation around to tulip growing. Eventually the tulip grower started to explain how he did it.

And this is what he said. 'You know my farm is overrun with rodents, thousands of them. I lay traps everywhere to catch them. If I didn't do that all the tulip bulbs would get eaten before they could flower. But then I've got all these little dead bodies to dispose of, so I cook them up and turn them into jam. But then no one will eat the jam, so I spread it on the fields. And it must be wonderful stuff, because it makes the tulips grow like anything.'

And his friend said, 'You know what, I don't believe a word of it. Tell me what you really do.' And the tulip grower said, 'Oh yeah? Everyone knows you get Tulips From Hamster Jam.'

RUNNING JOKES

A running joke is a joke that's repeated, with variations, through a piece of writing. The classic comedy movie *Airplane!* was stuffed with running gags, from 'Don't call me Shirley' (every time someone starts a sentence with 'Surely') to Ted Striker's 'drink problem' (he misses his mouth every time).

Running jokes can be used in any kind of comedy writing. Here's a small example from *The Inimitable Jeeves*, which starts:

The brother was a small round cove with a face rather like a sheep.

and a couple of pages later:

...and as for the brother, he looked like a sheep with a secret sorrow.

At this point the brother... gave a little cough, like a sheep caught in the mist on a mountain top.

THEMED JOKES

As well as taking a single joke and repeating it with variations, you can run a series of themed jokes through a piece. These are particularly useful in diary-format novels, where they create a feeling of continuity. For instance, in *The Secret Diary of Adrian Mole Aged 13¾*, Adrian repeatedly writes to the BBC and in *The Timewaster Diaries* Robin's wife Rita is constantly spraining her ankle.

Candy Guard, comic artist
(*Pond Life, The Observer*)

'The most common mistake new comedy writers make is: telling lies.'

Other joke formats

There are many formats for jokes and comedy generally. They provide a framework for the writer and an expectation for the listener.

Short joke templates

We've already looked at 'changing a light bulb' jokes and 'going into a bar' jokes. Here are a few more formats for short jokes, with examples.

Knock, knock

> 'Knock, knock.'
>
> 'Who's there?'
>
> 'Norma Lee.'
>
> 'Norma Lee who?'
>
> 'Norma Lee I have my key.'

Doctor, doctor

> 'Doctor doctor, I feel like a pack of cards.'
>
> 'Wait there and I'll deal with you later.'

Waiter

> 'Waiter, what's this fly doing in my soup?'
>
> 'Breast stroke?'

Confucius say

> 'Man who tell too many light-bulb jokes soon burn out.'

Murphy's Law

> If everything seems to be going well, you must have overlooked something.

What's the difference?

> What's the difference between roast beef and pea soup?
>
> Anyone can roast beef but no one can pee soup.

What do you get if you cross...

> What do you get if you cross a tourist and an elephant?
>
> Something that carries its own trunk.

Conundrums

In its narrowest meaning, a conundrum is a verbal puzzle that involves a pun:

> What is black and white and red all over? A newspaper. (red/read)

but it can also play with an idiom:

> Why don't cannibals eat clowns? Because they taste funny.

In its broader sense, a conundrum can be any kind of puzzle where the answer requires a degree of lateral thinking and it isn't even necessarily funny:

> Every day a man leaves his apartment on the 46th floor and rides the lift down to the first floor to go to work. Every evening he takes the lift up to the 38th floor, gets out and walks up the stairs for the remaining eight floors until he reaches the 46th floor. Why?

> Because he is too short to reach the lift buttons above 38.

And sometimes a conundrum is a question without an answer:

> Why are boxing rings square?

These kinds of questions are staple for stand-up comics, often in this rather tired format:

> If you want to turn off your computer, you have to press the start button. What's that all about, then?

Spoonerisms

These are named after the Reverend Spooner, a nineteenth-century cleric. He was teased for inadvertently swapping the initial letters of words to comic effect (although there is little evidence that he actually did so). For example:

> 'Well-boiled icicle' for 'well-oiled bicycle'

and one splendid set of three sentences:

> 'You have hissed all my mystery lectures. You have tasted a whole worm. Please leave Oxford on the next town drain.' (You have missed all my history lectures. You have wasted a whole term. Please leave Oxford on the next down train.)

More complicated spoonerisms play with syllables and entire words, such as:

> I'd rather have a bottle in front of me than a frontal lobotomy.

Occasionally this trick provides material for a cleverly written sketch – Benny Hill and the Two Ronnies both used it. It can also help convey obscenity without needing to use the taboo words.

Malapropisms

These are named after the character Mrs Malaprop from Sheridan's play *The Rivals*. She consistently uses words inappropriately, such as 'pineapple' instead of 'pinnacle'. More recently, George W. Bush has given comedians masses of similar material with his inability to find the right word, or even a real word:

'They misunderestimated me.'

Steve Delaney continues this type of comedy with his character Count Arthur Strong, who gets in a terrible muddle with words.

Tom Swifties

Tom Swifties started as a parody of a style used in a series of books from the early twentieth century. The idea is to use an adverb in a punning way:

'We must put the fire out,' he said heatedly.

'I twisted a muscle,' he said limply.

Sometimes you can get another layer with a pun in the adverb:

'I hear Elvis is dead,' she said expressly (Ex-Presley).

There are many variations on this basic theme, not all using adverbs:

'Mmm, a burger in a bun,' she said with relish.

Tom Swifties may seem too specialized to bother with, but writing them is another good way of training your comedy muscles. The basic jokes can sometimes be used to add texture to a comedy scenario. For instance, if you were writing about a disastrous barbeque you might find a use for 'heatedly' and 'with relish', especially if you had a character who was known for their feeble jokes.

Limericks

Limericks are simple five-line poems using an AABBA rhyme pattern. (This just means that all the 'A' lines must rhyme with one another and the 'B' lines must rhyme with one another). The first line is usually about the name of the subject or where they live:

There once was a woman from Ryde

Who ate some green apples and died.

The apples fermented

Inside the lamented

And made cider inside her inside.

Clerihews

The clerihew was invented by Edmund Clerihew Bentley. It consists of a four-line verse with the rhyme pattern AABB. The first line usually includes the subject's name and the third and fourth lines are longer than the first two. This irregularity adds to the comic effect:

Lesley Bown

Tried to write it all down

But when she needed a rhyme for Clerihew

She found that there were very few.

Where to next?

Where do jokes lead? Inevitably, to stand-up comedy. So that's where we're going next.

6

Stand-up

Stand-up is exactly what it sounds like – you stand up in front of an audience and make them laugh. As a writer, you have to decide whether to perform your own jokes or whether to work with a performer. Even if you don't see yourself as a performer, you'll learn a lot about stand-up if you have a go yourself. However you choose to do it, it's very important to get your routines in front of an audience to test them out.

In this chapter you will learn about the basics of stand-up comedy, how to write a stand-up routine and the differences between traditional and observational stand-up.

Watch a stand-up performance

Go to a live stand-up performance. Observe the audience and work out how the comic establishes a connection with them. Do they talk directly to audience members? Do they use local jokes? Do they try to get sympathy?

At a pinch, you can do this exercise by watching a recording at home.

Don't be afraid of the audience. They've turned up with the intention of enjoying themselves. They want to laugh, so they'll usually meet you more than halfway. Think about their concerns, their attitude to things when you're writing. This doesn't have to be about agreeing with or endorsing their attitude, it's much more about understanding it.

Some themes are universal. You can talk to any audience about old age, although you'd take a different perspective for teenagers compared with pensioners. Other themes are very specific. If the routine is for an audience of estate agents or cacti enthusiasts, then you can do jokes that only they would understand. You'd also need to do your research too of course.

Next, think about the performer, which means think about their on-stage character. Make contact with a stand-up who works locally, so that you can watch them performing. Try to meet them and learn as much as possible about their take on comedy. Ask who their comedy heroes are, and what inspires them. Make sure you understand how they like to open and close their routines and how they like to deal with hecklers.

Study a stand-up routine

Watch a recording of a stand-up routine. Watch it several times and make notes.

1 List the topics covered.
2 Note how the routine moves between topics.
3 Mark the laughs, big and small.

The basics of routining

When you're assembling a stand-up routine, aim for two or three laughs a minute – they won't all be big belly laughs. Start with something simple that doesn't require much of a set-up, so that the comic can get that all-important first laugh. It helps to choose something that the audience can connect with – it gets them on the comic's side. Later on, the routine can become more fantastical or surreal, but not with the opening gags.

Here are some useful tips for writing a routine:

1 First, choose an order for your routine – it can be chronological (e.g. from wedding to honeymoon) or anything else that makes sense.

2 Don't have similar types of joke too close together, and look at the pacing. Try to identify where the big laughs will fall and have smaller laughs on either side of them to create peaks and troughs. Always save the best joke and the biggest laugh for the end.

Key idea

Judging the size of the laughs isn't easy, but you'll learn a lot when you see the routine performed, or perform it yourself.

Focus point

Be sure to be there when your work is being performed and always be prepared to rewrite the next day.

GO WITH THE FLOW

There are ways of keeping the routine flowing. You can link groups of jokes on disparate topics by writing a joke that connects them (which is why you practised finding connections). The more subtly you insert links, the more spontaneous the routine will seem.

Reincorporation means mentioning something early on, moving on from it and then returning to it towards the end when the audience have forgotten about it. It can generate huge laughs if it's done well.

Early jokes can be used to set up the later ones, perhaps by establishing certain characteristics. For instance, the joke about eating steak to get more greens could be used to establish that the comic isn't into healthy eating, and it could lead on to jokes about environmental matters or political correctness, always with the comic going the unfashionable route.

 Kev F. Sutherland, comedian and comic artist (Beano, Marvel, Viz, etc.)

'Many, many scripts entered into The Sitcom Trials consist of talking heads wittering on, discussing events that happened in the past. This is rarely interesting. Conversely, that is all stand-up is, so you have to learn the difference between the disciplines.'

Traditional stand-up

Traditional stand-up routines are joke based. Some comics just tell one joke after another, while others pace the jokes with fillers.

Some of the examples in Chapter 5 can be turned into a short routine, even though they weren't written with that intention:

> When I was a teenager I had a terrible weight problem. I didn't just have puppy fat – if I sunbathed on the beach Greenpeace would send a crew to try and refloat me. Still, I did manage to find a husband. He was quite a guy. He had a mind like a steel trap – always closed. And boy, was he mean. Never spent a penny if he could avoid it. Well, he believed that money can't buy you happiness. I said to him, oh yeah? If money can't buy you happiness, how come we have to pay for chocolate?

At the beginning this needs more jokes, either about puppy fat or other aspects of teenage angst. When it moves on to the mean husband it looks more promising, and it could lead to a rant about marriage or maybe a series of money jokes.

Another way to create a traditional routine is to choose a topic and make a list of items connected with the topic. Take each item and break it down into subheadings. Then use the techniques you've already learned to generate jokes. Once you've produced a lot of jokes, many more than you need, choose the best three from each group.

Traditional comics often have a set format for their opening – for years Ken Dodd has used 'What a wonderful day for...' Many traditional comics also like to finish with a song, a piece of advice or some homespun philosophy.

Observational stand-up

Writing a routine for an observational comic requires a different technique because it's based on observing the quirks of life that we all share but haven't necessarily noticed. Observations like this connect the comic with the audience and produce the kind of laughter that is more like a groan of recognition.

 Key idea

The real belly laughs come from playing with the observation, taking it beyond reality to madness or fantasy.

One obvious potential problem for professional comedians is that they quite quickly find that they don't have much in common with their audience. Working at night, sleeping during the day, on the road many weeks of the year – this is not a typical lifestyle. Some years ago, Jasper Carrott built an entire routine around the fact that his increasing affluence was changing his relationship with his audience, but it would soon get tiresome if everyone did this. As a writer, you may be able to help the performer stay in touch with normality.

The first step is to make the observations. You can do these at random, for instance:

When men are watching TV, they can't hear you talk to them.

If you want to stop your computer, click Start.

Dogs have to pee every 30 seconds on a walk.

Men like to rearrange the dishes in the dishwasher.

Or you can choose a topic and see how many observations you can make round it:

Dogs have to pee every 30 seconds on a walk.

The nastier the dog, the more likely the owner is to say, 'That's just his way of being friendly.'

Sometimes his way of being friendly is to hump your leg.

People who kiss their dogs on the mouth never seem to realize that the last thing the dog kissed was another dog's bottom.

Random observations

Write down your own random observations about life.

Next, look through the observations and see what catches your eye. Let's start with the first one about men watching TV. Make notes around the topic:

Men – can't scratch their heads and eat a boiled egg at the same time. Can't talk while they're watching TV.

Multitasking has been in the news, because research has shown that women actually are better at it.

When kids do their homework in front of the TV, are they multitasking?

Women multitasking – cooking, cleaning, helping with homework, soothing the baby and holding down a career. Shopping lists, booking holidays, ferrying kids to ballet and football. Putting on make-up at the traffic lights, ordering groceries online in the lunch hour.

What about jobs that men used to do – cutting the grass, servicing machinery or changing a tap washer? Do they still do them?

Expand an observation

Choose one of your observations and expand it.

Now make some choices, based on the audience and the performer. Let's say that this set is for a comic who uses the voice of an older woman, a man-hating cleaning lady with a lazy husband. She doesn't have a career and has grown-up kids. The audience is likely to be in the same age group, so we need to edit out any topics that don't fit.

Get focused

Decide what sort of audience and performer you're writing for (real or imagined) and edit your notes accordingly.

The next task is to arrange an order:

a Introduce multitasking – new scientific research
b Talk about it in a fairly realistic way – things women can do which men can't do
c Extend into the realms of fantasy – a woman still multitasking while having sex.

Get organized

Put your notes in order.

Finally, write it up. This routine is for a clearly defined comedy character with a specific voice, which has to be taken into consideration.

Then edit, rewrite and maybe end up with this:

I've got nothing against men, mind, but I seen in the papers, them scientists has worked out that men can only do one thing at a time, while women, right, women are what's called multifunctional.

Now what that means is a women can cook the breakfast, delouse the dog, change the spark plug on the motor mower and do the kids' homework all at the same time. But men can only do one the thing. And if he's scratching his head, well, don't expect him to do nothing else. Blimey, we didn't need no scientist to tell us that, did we? I think we'd worked that one out, hadn't we, girls?

And I don't want to go on about sex, I leave that to the Women's Institute, but you know what it's like, don't you, you've got the man shouting, "Yes yes!" while the women is getting on with her orgasm, writing a shopping list, *and* trying to decide whether to go to Venice or Venezuela for next year's holiday. Oh, and if it's Monday morning she's probably changing the sheets and if it's Saturday she'll be stripping the wallpaper off with a chisel, ready to start decorating.

Create an observational routine

Write a short routine based on your observations.

As we've already seen, with joke-based stand-up you aim for three jokes on a topic, and the same concept applies to observational stand-up. In other words, that was enough about multitasking – time to move on to the next topic, which in this case was triggered by a news item about mapping the human genome. The same process of making notes and choosing an order produces these opening remarks on the topic:

> I seen on the Internet that them scientists have mapped the genome. I can see you're surprised I use the Internet. Well, I am one of them silver sufferers. You see, it's us women what are into this hands-on technology. Men buy the computers, right, and they boast about the size of their rams and hard drives or whatever, but it's us women what work out how to use 'em. I tell you, I roar down that information superhighway so fast it's a wonder I haven't been booked for speeding.

With one more topic – holidays – the process can be repeated to produce a short set. An entry-level set for a comedy club is three to five minutes, so aim for that to start with. Longer sets are 10 or 20 minutes, which is more of a writing challenge – it doesn't work if you just pad out a short set.

In fact, this set was written for a real performer, who was able to test it on a willing group, when it was immediately obvious that links were needed between the topics. For instance, the link between multitasking and the human genome went like this:

> And talking of chisels – don't men ever go mad if you use one instead of a screwdriver? I mean, what's the big deal, they look the same don't they? Anyway, I was only scraping out the oven, no call for him making all that fuss.

> Course, he still thinks that sort of thing is woman's work, along with hoovering, gardening and servicing the car. So don't give me all that New Man stuff. He says he done his bit when he wrote the cheque for the dishwasher. So why is it that, as fast as I put the plates in, he takes 'em out again and just ever so slightly rearranges them? What's that all about, then?

> Of course, we're told it's all in the genes…

Creating links

Create links between your topics so that your routine has flow.

Double acts and impressionists

A traditional double act consists of a straight person and a funny person – usually men of course. Morecambe and Wise took this to its peak, and recently it's all but disappeared. Double acts now are more likely to consist of multi-talented performers who adopt a range of characters, so that writing for them is mainly about sketch writing. If you're interested in writing for a ventriloquist, treat it like a double act.

Impressionists need scripts that are funny, sharp and in character, or rather characters. You'll need an understanding of the performer's talents and limitations, and an insight into the subjects of the impressions.

Workshop

Choose one of your routines, either traditional or observational, for this workshop.

1 Read it out loud, more than once, and fine-tune it to suit your particular delivery.
2 If possible, record yourself, sound only. Fine-tune again.
3 If possible, film yourself. Fine-tune again.
4 Perform it to a small audience who won't be too judgemental – friends or family. Fine-tune again in response to their feedback.

Each time you fine-tune, ask yourself:
- Have I got a mix of big laughs and small laughs?
- Is my opening laugh based on a simple accessible joke?
- Have I managed about three jokes on each topic?
- Have I got good links between the topics?
- Have I used reincorporation?
- Is the best joke at the end?

Where to next?

Now you're going to learn how to create characters for comedy, starting with the simple characters needed for short forms of comedy.

7

Simple characters and situations

Once you move beyond writing jokes, you'll find that character underpins every aspect of comedy writing. You've already seen that the on-stage character of a stand-up comic has a direct bearing on the type of routine that will work for them.

In this chapter you will learn to create simple comedy characters, including stock characters and basic character types that work well in comedy. You will find out how to create a comic voice for your characters and how conflict underpins character in comedy. You will discover that sources for characters are all around you and how to make them funny, as well as how to create situations with comedy potential.

Creating comedy characters

A lot of comedy uses very simple characters, often quite stereotypical, because they're easily recognized. Even the more unusual characters generally have a dominant characteristic that can be presented to the audience quickly and simply. Whether you're writing humorous prose or a routine for performance, the same guidelines apply to creating characters, although the ways in which you convey the information to your audience will differ.

Most stand-ups are an exaggerated version of themselves, but a smaller number of stand-ups create an entire fictional character. (Who would have thought that ignorant, bigoted Al Murray, the pub landlord, was in reality Oxford-educated Alastair Murray?) If you're writing for either type of stand-up, you'll need to constantly check that you're staying within the boundaries of their on-stage character. If you work with someone who's at the start of their career, then you may be able to help them develop that character.

 ## Key idea

Stand-up is not a question of getting up on stage and just being yourself.

 ## Get the style right

Take one of your earlier jokes and rewrite it in the style of your favourite stand-up. Then rewrite it for your least favourite stand-up.

The same applies if you're writing a humorous article for a magazine or writing a first-person short story or novel: the voice you use will either be an exaggeration of your normal voice or else you'll create an entirely new character and write in their voice.

Here's me using a version of my own voice for an article about why I bought a motorcaravan:

> When I first met Mike it was wintertime and everything looked perfect. We agreed about all the important things in life: money, politics, and how to spend your holidays – camping of course.

Come the spring I, as usual, put my tent up in the garden to air it, and that's when the trouble started. 'I hate frame tents,' Mike declared, rummaging in a carrier bag. 'We'll have to use this.' He threw on to the grass something that looked like a scruffy, faded, orange handkerchief. 'No way', I told him, 'am I sleeping in something a passing drunk might blow his nose on.'

And here's me, writing on the same topic, using the voice of an invented posh totty character who is definitely nothing like me at all:

However many berths one has in one's motoring caravan it is simply foolish to allow the butler to use one of them. The thing to do is to send the man on ahead with a pup tent, which will be quite adequate for his needs. With judicious planning, it should be possible for him to serve one's breakfast at home and be on the camping site ready with luncheon just as one arrives.

Eric Chappell, writer

'Always remember that character comes first and situation comes second.'

Conflict

Key idea

The most important thing is to give the character some sort of conflict.

There are three different levels of conflict and as a writer you can use any or all of them. They are inner conflict, conflict with other people and conflict with society. The first two types form the bulk of comedy within our culture, because most people can identify with them.

1   **Inner conflict:** This is when a character wants two different, and conflicting, things out of life. For example, Basil Fawlty is a social climber who wants to mix with a better class of person, but he also wants to be affluent, and making money can be a grubby business.

2   **Conflict with other people:** In *Black Books*, Bernard Black is at odds with everyone, including his two friends. A lot of comedy is written round the concept of a central, slightly odd, character

who has no inner conflict but who is constantly in conflict with the people around them. Mr Pooter, the main character in *The Diary of a Nobody*, is quite sure that he knows how life should be; his problem is that other people rarely agree with him. Mr Bean is a similar type of character.

3 **Conflict with society:** This type of conflict is clearly useful when a writer wants to make a political point and is more common in societies with high political tension. Tom Sharpe's 1970s novels *Indecent Exposure* and *Riotous Assembly* are about life in South Africa in the days of apartheid. He mocks all the races caught up in the regime, while also making the serious point that everyone is diminished by it. In the UK we had *Citizen Smith*, a 1970s sitcom about a young left-winger who is at odds with the comfortable suburban life that surrounds him, and who wants to start a revolution. However, most of the comedy arises from his incompetence and inability to have any effect on the world he so dislikes.

Stock characters

Stock characters are the ones we all recognize instantly: the tart with the heart of gold, the dithery vicar, the power-crazed traffic warden, and so on. Outside comedy it is generally thought to be undesirable to use such characters and to be a sign of lazy writing, but in comedy stock characters are extremely useful.

 Focus point

Jokes, quickies and sketches all rely heavily on stock characters because they are instantly recognizable and they behave in ways that the audience expects.

As a writer you have two choices. You can go with the stereotype and get your comedy from exaggerating it beyond the expectations of the audience. Characters like Armstrong and Miller's Two Menopausal Ladies, with their violently exaggerated mood swings, fall into this category.

Alternatively, you can undermine expectations by having a character behave in the opposite way from the stereotype. This works very well, because the opposite way is bound to be incongruous – for instance, in the Lumberjack Song, the Monty Python team created a manly looking lumberjack who yearned to wear women's underwear. More recently, Catherine Tate's Nan Taylor is the opposite of what we'd expect from a grandmother.

Using stock characters

Make a list of ten stock characters and decide how you'd exaggerate and undermine each one.

Character types

Only one step removed from stock characters, there are certain basic character types that work particularly well in comedy and recur again and again. Stand-up comedians often base their persona on one of these basic comedy characters.

- **The deadpan:** Nothing but nothing will cause this character to bend a face muscle. Jack Dee has perfected this character.
- **The fish out of water:** ET and Crocodile Dundee are characters adrift in a strange culture. As well as giving comedy value as they find their way around the world, making mistakes due to their ignorance, they are also a good hook on which to hang a story.
- **The innocent:** Often also a klutz (see below), this type can be simply a childlike innocent constantly bewildered by his or her failures. These characters can also bring an offbeat perspective on the world – for example Father Dougal in *Father Ted*.
- **The jester:** Many stand-up comedians have taken the simple jester option in the past – Arthur Askey, for instance – although the character is less popular in these cynical times.
- **The klutz:** A childlike character who keeps getting everything wrong. At first he can't get the lid off the ketchup, then it suddenly shoots off, spraying him with red goo. He licks it off his clothing and ends up eating his tie. This type works well in physical comedy, for example *Mr Bean*.
- **The know-it-all:** At the opposite end of the spectrum from the innocent, this character is sure they know what's what. Del Boy in *Only Fools and Horses* is a good example. Del Boy has other, more lovable qualities, but this isn't essential, for instance David Brent in *The Office*.
- **The loser:** The loser is particularly popular in UK comedy – Tony Hancock developed the template for this on radio and TV. However, it features in American movies, too – for instance, The Dude in *The Big Lebowski*.

- **The neurotic:** The neurotic worries about everything under the sun – Woody Allen has perfected this schtick.
- **The social climber:** The opposite of the vulgarian (see below), this character tries far too hard to be refined. Examples abound in class-obsessed UK comedy: examples are Basil Fawlty, Hyacinth Bouquet and Harold Steptoe, among many others.
- **The vulgarian:** This character pays no attention to social niceties or other people's needs. He takes the ketchup from the next table, returns it empty, helps himself to a chip from a child's plate and is chased down the road by the irate father. Examples include both Richie and Eddie in *Bottom*.

Workshop

Someone goes into a shop to buy a newspaper. You have two characters, the shopper and the shop assistant. How would the scene pan out with the following pairings?
- Deadpan/jester
- Fish out of water/neurotic
- Innocent/know-it-all
- Klutz/loser
- Social climber/vulgarian.

Write the first few lines of dialogue between each pair (don't worry about a plot for this, just focus on the characters). With each pairing, try the characters in both roles.
- Which characters are funniest as the shopper?
- Which characters are funniest as the shop assistant?

Sources for original characters

Characters need a spark of originality, and for that reason you should look all around you to find them, although no doubt you'll come to realize that most of the characters you create do fall into one of the above types.

PEOPLE WATCHING

If you observe people when you're out and about, you'll notice all sorts of interesting behaviours that may kick-start a character for you. Look also at people you already know.

Practise description

Write a brief description of a person you've observed in real life.

1 Describe their appearance, their body language and their clothes.

2 Describe their character, including their vices and virtues.

3 Make it as accurate as possible.

4 Decide what you would need to change to make the character funny.

PLAYS, MOVIES, TV, NOVELS

You will be influenced by the characters created by other writers – it's inevitable – although there's no excuse for shameless copying. Your source character doesn't have to come from a comedy. You might choose to write a modern take on pompous Pooter from *The Diary of a Nobody*, but equally you might create a comic version of Miss Marple or Frodo.

Making serious characters funny

Make a list of five serious characters from other writers' work and explore their comic potential. What would you have to change to make them funny?

WELL-KNOWN PEOPLE

There is plenty of comedy to be gained from writing about real-life figures. If they are still alive or only recently dead, you will have to consider legal issues and the libel laws in particular. Historical figures, though, are fair game. You can either use the received wisdom about them (for instance, Henry VIII as both fat and cruel) or create entirely new characters for them.

For example, Sue Limb created *The Wordsmiths at Gorsemere* for Radio 4, a parody of the lives of Wordsworth and Coleridge together with their families, friends and hangers on, many of whom are also well known in their own right.

Using a well-known person

Take any well-known figure and explore their comic potential:

- Write out a simple description of what is known about them.
- Look at how the facts could be changed to create comedy.

Realism

A lot of comedy arises from exaggerating reality, and characters are no exception. However, you have a choice in how far you take this. Ben Harper in *My Family* was a very slightly exaggerated character – I suspect most of us know someone who is quite a lot like him. Basil Fawlty is more exaggerated, and yet many of us have been in hotels and restaurants that are not too far removed from Fawlty Towers. Douglas Reynholm, the boss of Reynholm Industries in *The IT Crowd*, is exaggerated beyond any connection with reality. Of course, there are various kinds of realism – for example, Bollo the talking gorilla in *The Mighty Boosh* is completely unreal in one sense, but has an instantly recognizable human character.

Ann Gawthorpe, writer

'The most common mistake new comedy writers make is making a character behave uncharacteristically just to get a laugh. There should be a good and logical reason for a character to behave outside their normal parameters.'

Characteristics

In comedy writing, characteristics are very important and can generate a lot of laughs. Characteristics are all the things that are on the surface of a character – how they look, move, speak and dress.

It's a good idea to visualize your characters physically. If you're writing for performance, you may find that an actor is cast who looks quite different from your mental image and you will need to accept that this happens. If you're lucky, the actor will take over and make the character live. While you're writing, though, you will need a picture in your head. If you're writing for a specific performer, you will need to use their physical traits and mannerisms, but otherwise it's up to you.

You'll be making certain choices for the character, regarding appearance, speech and behaviour. You can, of course deliberately take them out of the bounds you've created for them, but there has to be a reason. If an immaculately dressed character is suddenly scruffy or a softly spoken one starts shouting, this will signal to the audience that something major has happened.

Alan Ayckbourn, director and playwright

'The most common mistake new comedy writers make is trying to be funny.'

Ray Cooney, playwright

'The most common mistake new comedy writers make is trying to be funny.'

Stock situations

Stock situations are extremely useful to the comedy writer. At the most basic level, a cartoonist only has to draw a palm tree and a little hump and we know straight away that it's a 'stranded on a desert island' joke. Stock situations occur over and over again in sketches, quickies and sitcoms as well as cartoons.

Here are some other examples of stock situations:

- Angels on a cloud
- In the doctor's waiting room
- Couple sitting on a sofa
- In a restaurant
- In a shop
- In a pub
- In the office.

Using stock situations

Choose one of the stock situations listed above and write or draw ten jokes for it.

Focus point

Using stock situations takes away the need for an elaborate set-up and puts the audience straight into the action. More unusual situations need careful setting up, which is easier in a longer piece. (See Chapter 10 for more about setting up situations.)

Situations also need comedy potential. On the whole, that means choosing places where people interact and where there is the potential for conflict. That's why all forms of customer services are so fruitful – shops, reception areas, car salerooms and so on.

Unusual situations

Make a list of ten unusual situations with comedy potential. Look for:

- potential for interactions
- potential for conflict
- potential for frustration.

Where to next?

Now that you can create simple characters, you can try putting them into the situations that lead to quickies and sketches.

8

Quickies and sketches

A sketch is like a long joke, and usually runs for between two and eight minutes, whereas a quickie is more like a one-liner with just a set-up and a punchline. There is no room in either for unnecessary words or lines, so creating them offers excellent writing practice.

Both require simple situations that an audience can understand instantly, and a small number of characters. Characters for quickies are very simply drawn. For sketches, each character will need a single dominant characteristic and some sort of conflict that will drive the sketch forward.

In this chapter you will learn how to write quickies and basic sketches using various different tried and tested formats.

Kev F. Sutherland, comedian and comic artist (Beano, Marvel, Viz, etc.)

'The most common mistake new comedy writers make is writing stuff that can't be performed. Whether you're writing sketches, stand-up, plays, TV or sitcom, you're writing material to be performed and you are always going to need to keep the audience's attention. Reading your work out loud or, better, getting someone else to read it, can help.'

Quickies

Quickies are often just a joke acted out, and they usually end with a blackout (on stage) or a camera cut or pullback (on TV). The pullback reveals a visual punchline. Because they are so quick, they must be simple and cheap to do – with no fancy special effects. There are endless variations to be had from two people talking:

Boy: They said in Assembly taking E destroys your memory, like.

Girl: What destroys your memory?

Boy: I dunno, who told you that?

Girl: Told me what?

You can also write linked quickies, where a whole series of characters comes into the same situation, with a bigger laugh for each one. If they are performed consecutively, it's more like a sketch than a series of quickies.

 Key idea

There's no time to develop characters with quickies, so you need a very clear understanding of each one and you need to be able to convey that to the audience.

To write a quickie, start with an easily recognized situation and introduce one or two characters. Use the same techniques to generate quickies as you used for short jokes, but remember to think visually.

Write quickies

Write a two-character quickie for each of the stock situations listed in Chapter 7:

- Angels on a cloud
- In the doctor's waiting room
- Couple sitting on a sofa
- In a restaurant
- In a shop
- In a pub
- In the office.

Sometimes quickies don't need dialogue at all:

Scene: supermarket car park

We see an elderly lady struggling with a full trolley. She spots a handsome young customer-care assistant and waves him over. He pushes her trolley to the car. She opens the car, pushes him in and drives off, leaving the trolley.

Write no-dialogue quickies

For each of the situations on the list given in the previous exercise, write a two-character quickie with no dialogue.

Remember that, even if you're writing for radio, you'll still need to create pictures for the listeners. In fact, the visual side of radio comedy is worth exploiting to the full, because you can be as surreal and illogical as you like:

Police who found 66 pounds of cocaine in the nose cone of a jumbo jet became suspicious after it refused to land and kept circling the airport making whooping noises.

A blind man has paddled a canoe round Britain in five months. He would've been quicker, but the dog kept chasing Channel Ferries.

Once you have a good set-up for a quickie, see whether you can get more than one joke out of it by doing a series. For instance, an office setting is simple to create and has endless possibilities:

Scene: man and woman both working at their desks

Man: Oi! Sellotape!

Woman throws it over to him

Woman: I want that back. I know what you're like. Take the blouse off my back given half a chance, you would.

Man: Oh, stop your moaning.

Woman: Me! What about you... (*phone rings, she answers it*) Hello – Society of Friends.

Once the principle is established, the joke can be reworked for any number of office settings. For instance:

- people playing = Child Psychiatry
- people struggling to add up coffee money = Institute of Accountants
- people asleep = Energy Saving Trust
- people getting lost on the way to their desks = Institute of Navigation.

Try to raise the comedy stakes a little for each one, and save a good one for last:

Scene: man and woman both working at their desks

Man: So I came off the motorway and got onto the old A38, completely empty, not a car in sight, and I made up all the time I'd lost, even stopped at a little country pub for lunch, lovely it was, just like a place I went to on holiday in Devon a couple of years ago, no, tell a lie, it was the North York Moors, wonderful inglenook fireplace, middle of nowhere, right off the beaten track, I was staying a few miles away in a little B and B, recommended to me by my mother's cousin, don't know if I mentioned her, she's got a wooden leg, married a chap from Derby, Edwina Currie used to be her MP, of course she's from Liverpool originally, I went to Liverpool once...

(*phone rings, woman answers it*)

Woman: Hello – Rambler's Association.

 Variations on quickies

See how many variations you can find on one of your quickies.

Sketches

Traditionally, sketches are based on one idea and tell the story of a single incident. As the sketch unfolds, there are several laughs building to the punchline. The set-up for a sketch is known as the premise and it needs to be established very quickly. The premise is important – the whole sketch hangs from it – so it must be strong enough to drive the action but, equally, not too big: don't choose something that needs a half-hour sitcom or a full-length novel to do it justice.

Focus point

Once the action has started, there should be a moment when the audience knows that things are going to go wrong.

On a practical note, remember that sketches have a limited budget. A simple set is all you can expect on stage, and for TV don't write in special effects, location filming, night filming or anything else that will be expensive.

Sue Limb, comedy writer (Dulcie Domum, *Up the Garden Path, The Wordsmiths at Gorsemere*)

'*My favourite comedy comes from characters passionately engaged in serious stuff and not realizing that they're being funny.*'

SKETCH FORMATS

As well as the basic sketch, there are several tried and tested formats:

Travelling in time

Either project into the future, or go backwards into history. Always pick something that the audience is going to recognize instantly – Queen Victoria talking to Disraeli rather than Tennyson talking to his wife (unless, of course, there has recently been a successful costume drama about Tennyson, putting him back in the public eye).

You can also use anachronisms, where a character takes twenty-first-century attitudes into the past. This is the basis for Armstrong and Miller's Second World War airmen who use current street jargon.

Send-up or parody

Again, this has to be instantly recognizable – a current movie or TV programme or a celebrity in the news.

Reversal

This basically means having characters do the opposite of what the audience expects. Put a stereotypical character in an unfamiliar situation – for instance, a doctor at home talking to his wife as if she were a patient.

Writing sketches

There are two basic ways of writing sketches. If you already have an idea for a complete sketch, all you have to do is write it out and then edit and polish it – which is still quite a lot of work. More often than not, however, you'll have only the vaguest idea or even no idea at all, in which case you'll have to start from scratch.

 Key idea

The techniques you learned for joke writing will stand you in good stead for writing sketches.

THE SITUATION AND CHARACTERS

Let's look at the detail of writing a sketch. This one is going to be about funerals. The most easily recognized funeral situation is mourners standing round the open grave, but that requires location filming and in any case most people are cremated these days. We could set it in the church or crematorium but those are quite complicated sets. For a one-off sketch, the actual funeral parlour is the easiest to set up, and this would also work on stage.

As for characters, obviously there are the bereaved and the undertakers. We could consider new staff in the undertakers, comically inappropriate, or a customer who is under some sort of misapprehension and isn't actually bereaved at all. To keep it simple,

I'll choose an undertaker and a customer who is there to deal with some aspect of the funeral process.

Choose situation and characters

Choose a situation for your sketch and decide what roles the two characters will have.

GENERATING IDEAS

Once you have the situation and characters, make lists of everything you can think of relating to them, exactly as you did for joke writing.

Focus point

The comedy must come from either the characters or the situation (or both), and the lists will stop you being distracted as you write.

My list is:

> Funeral, undertaker, hearse, black, flowers, different funeral packages, corpse, embalming, urn, ashes, coffins, reincarnation, heaven and hell, headstone, memorial and so on.

Next, take each word on your list and look for connections, opposites, alternative uses, visual jokes, word plays and clichés. For instance:

> Funeral – ceremony, mourners, procession, burial, cremation, wedding, christening, gone to a better place, funeral contains the syllable 'fun', arguing over the will and so on.

Spend a little time thinking about the jokes that these generate. This will help you get right inside the topic, and some of them will end up in the sketch. There are plenty of funeral jokes:

> One Saturday afternoon, a funeral procession passes the football ground. A fan takes his hat off and bows his head. His friend says, 'That's a really nice gesture.' 'It's the least I can do, says the bloke "She was a good wife to me for over 40 years.

Engraved on a headstone: 'Here lies an Atheist, all dressed up and nowhere to go.'

A passenger in a taxi taps the driver on the shoulder to ask him a question. The driver screams, loses control of the cab, nearly hits a bus, drives up the kerb and stops just inches from a large plate-glass window. He says to the passenger, 'I'm sorry, you scared the daylights out of me. Today is my first day driving a cab... I've been driving a hearse for the last 25 years.'

ASKING THE RIGHT QUESTIONS

Once you've warmed up your comedy muscles with jokes around the topic, move on to the sketch. The most important questions to ask are 'What can go wrong?' and 'What if...?'. Ask those questions about everything on your lists and then look through them for funny items that hang nicely together.

The answer to the question 'What can go wrong at a funeral?' is 'Almost anything', although by confining ourselves to the funeral parlour we can't, for instance, use the old joke of a drunk falling into the grave – unless, of course, it's described after the event. In any case, because funerals are important and emotional affairs, people generally want them to run smoothly – so anything going wrong produces a heightened response. Another list is called for:

- Someone could have fallen in the grave.
- The undertaker could be drunk.
- The undertaker could be working his notice and be in the mood for trouble.
- The family could fall out over what they want.
- The wife and the mistress could both turn up at the funeral parlour.
- The coffin could fall to bits.

Now for the 'what ifs'. Don't be tempted to overlap with the first question (e.g. what if the undertaker was drunk?). This is your chance to explore connections and reach for the bizarre:

- What if the undertaker had a second job as a strippergram?
- What if the funeral parlour was being redecorated?
- What if business was quiet and they were using the hearse to sell ice cream?
- What if the customer was looking for a buy-one-get-one-free deal?
- What if the customer was a gangster looking for a bulk discount?
- What if the undertaker really wanted to be a lumberjack?

By now, something should be leaping out at you. If it isn't, then keep going with more lists, jokes and questions. In this example, I keep being drawn back to one thing – that the first syllable of funeral is 'fun'. This prompts more list making for ways of connecting funerals to fun:

- tap dancing on the coffin
- sawing the coffin in half
- party in the church
- the dead parrot sketch,
- pallbearers dressed as clowns
- Chapel of Jest.

FINE-TUNING THE CHARACTERS

It's time to think more about the characters. If you're writing for specific performers, you'll know about their strengths and weaknesses and that will have a bearing on the characters you create for them. In the case of the funeral sketch, it looks as if the comedy is going to arise out of the connection between funerals and fun, so the characters need to be fairly straightforward.

Focus point

If the situation is inherently funny, have a least one character that is unaware of this. If the situation is straightforward, then at least one character has to be funny.

There's always a danger of overloading a sketch. So how about an undertaker who appears stereotypically solemn and a little pompous, while at the same time treating fun funerals as completely normal, and a customer who is outraged at the idea but who is struggling to maintain her dignity at a difficult time? Is she the bereaved person? Is she arranging the funeral, or has she come in afterwards to pay the bill, or maybe pick up the ashes?

FINING-TUNING THE SITUATION

The situation before a funeral is far more tense than afterwards and would probably produce many comic possibilities, but we'd be in danger of poking fun at bereaved peoples' suffering. That would make for some fairly black comedy. Let's set the sketch after the funeral, when someone comes along to pay the bill.

The next task is to choose from your various lists. Look for at least three good jokes, and work out an order that will save the best till last.

Mike Vardy, TV director

'The most common mistake new comedy writers make is trying to get established characters to fit a plot that's unsuitable for them.'

Workshop

In this workshop you're going to do all the preparatory work for your sketch.

1 Make lists of everything you can think of relating to the situation and characters you've chosen.
2 Look for connections, opposites, alternative uses, visual jokes, word play and clichés.
3 Look for the jokes relating to the situation.
4 Ask, 'What can go wrong?'
5 Ask, 'What if...?'
6 Decide what's leaping out at you and develop it.
7 Make decisions about your characters. Give each one a dominant characteristic, and make sure that there is a strong contrast between them.
8 Choose items from your lists that will hang together to make your sketch.

PLOTTING YOUR SKETCH

Does a sketch need a plot? Just a little one. The simplest plot consists of three elements. First there is the set-up, or basic situation, then the trigger that sets events in motion, and finally the pay-off that resolves things. In other words, it's a lot like joke writing, and now you'll be glad you practised those skills.

So, once you've chosen the best jokes and looked at an order for them, consider what story they are going to tell. For the funeral sketch we'll have a simple linear plot – a woman comes in to pay her bill and it all unfolds from there.

 # Key idea

Keep it very simple – a sketch can't bear the weight of a complicated storyline.

WRITING A DRAFT

We already have the set-up of someone turning up to pay the bill for a funeral. The opening needs to swiftly set the scene:

A woman enters a funeral parlour.

Undertaker: May one be of assistance?

Woman: Um... yes... it's a bit awkward.

Undertaker: Modom has come to make arrangements for the dear departed? Rest assured, we are professionals.

Woman: No, no, it's not that...

Undertaker: Modom is aware that this is a funeral parlour?

Woman: (*Angry*) Is it? Are you sure?(*Makes an effort at self-control. Produces a piece of paper*). Actually, it's about this bill of yours...

This is the moment when the audience knows something is wrong – the trigger, or 'Uh-oh' moment.

The Undertaker is unperturbed.

Undertaker: (*taking the bill from her*) Ah, yes. Funeral of Mr Johnson. I take it Modom is here on behalf of Mrs Johnson?

Woman: Yes. She's my aunt. She couldn't come. She's a bit upset, you see.

Undertaker: Quite understandable. The grieving widow.

Woman: Not about that. Well, naturally she is upset about that, we all are, and then there was the funeral, that was quite distressing, and then when the bill came it was the last straw. It is a lot of money.

Undertaker: Mrs Johnson requested our top-of-the-range funeral. The Jeeves.

And this is the moment when the audience start to get a clue about what is going on. Jeeves is a very odd name for a funeral package, and we can reasonably expect the majority of people to make the connection with Jeeves and Wooster.

Woman: Yes. You see, she is rather elderly. I'm not sure that she entirely understood the, er, the implications.

Undertaker: And then there is the extra charge for the services of the embalmer. Did you view the deceased in our Chapel of Jest?

Now the audience should be in no doubt, assuming the performer has clear diction and puts enough weight on the word 'jest'.

Get going on your sketch

Now that you've made all your basic decisions, you can decide on the plot and start writing (and decisions can always be changed as you write).

- Create a simple plot for your sketch.
- Write the opening, with the set-up and the 'Uh-oh' moment.
- Finish the opening section of your sketch, to the point where the set-up is fully established.

Time for me to get into the meat of the sketch and slot in the various jokes:

Woman: Yes. Quite a shock.

Undertaker: So very lifelike. One almost expects the deceased to leap out of the coffin...

Woman: ...and say 'Mr Grimsdale!'

Undertaker: Ah yes, you had the Norman Wisdom. Very impressive.

Woman: Considering my uncle was six foot three and sixteen stone.

Undertaker: A triumph of the embalmer's art. Only possible when expense is no object.

Woman: It certainly wasn't cheap. And did we really need two priests for the service?

Undertaker: That is standard with the Jeeves. (*Woman looks puzzled.*) For the dead parrot sketch at the altar? (*Does a bad imitation of John Cleese*) 'This is an ex-parrot'?

Woman: (*not amused*) Yes. I was there. I think we'd have preferred it without the, er, frills.

Undertaker: Is Modom referring to our basic funeral, the Coco? It lacks the richness of the Jeeves, but the priest does wear a red nose and a revolving bow tie instead of his dog collar. A little obvious, perhaps, but most effective for a certain class of person.

Woman: It's just that it's not what we were expecting.

Undertaker: No? Surely Mrs Johnson understood the nature of our service to the bereaved? (*He reveals a poster on the wall, which reads 'We put the FUN back in FUNERAL'.*)

Woman: My aunt just wanted to do the best for her husband.

Undertaker: Quite so, Modom. The Jeeves was clearly the most suitable. Everything of the best. Finest mahogany coffin, very solid…

Woman: …that's true. The poor chap had quite a struggle to saw it in half. (*She takes out her credit cards.*) Look, I just want to pay the bill and forget about the whole thing. How much altogether?

Undertaker: That all depends on Modom's final decision. Regarding the ashes? (*He produces three identical urns from beneath the counter.*)

Woman: Which one is it?

Undertaker: That one. (*He takes the lid off, shows her the ashes, replaces the lid.*) Keep your eye on it. (*He swaps them round rapidly.*) Choose one.

Woman: Er… that one?

Undertaker: Sure?

Woman: Yes. No. Oh, that one. (*She opens an urn. A boxing glove on a spring pops out.*)

Undertaker: Modom wasn't paying attention, was Modom? It's this one, of course. (*He gives her the correct urn.*) We can arrange disposal if required.

ENDING A SKETCH

The biggest problems for most sketch writers are the pay-off and the ending. Even classic sketches often don't end especially well. For example, Monty Python's wonderful Lumberjack sketch ends fairly weakly with the girlfriend running off in tears. The psychopathic barber who wants to be a lumberjack was a great (and rather complicated) premise, but the ending was problematic.

If you watch a few classic sketches (such as The Two Ronnies' 'Fork Handles', Victoria Wood's 'Two Soups' and so on), you'll see that there are big laughs all the way through and quite often a smaller laugh at the end, but the ending is almost always a surprise – just enough to create the last laugh and round the sketch off.

Key idea

The key to the surprise at the end is that it is both logical and unpredictable – yes, that's right, just like joke writing.

At the end of 'Two Soups', the surprise is that the elderly waitress, who has seemed so subservient and willing to oblige, swears when she doesn't get a tip. And yet this is logical, too, because she must have had so many dissatisfied customers who didn't tip her that she's bound to have grown grumpy about it.

Another option for the ending is to come full circle and return to the beginning of the sketch.

A series of sketches that feature the same characters can all have the same ending. For instance, many of *Little Britain's* Vicky Pollard sketches end with the line 'Don't go giving me evils' – her ultimate riposte to whichever authority figure is trying to sort her out.

This is the end of the 'Funeral Fun' sketch:

> Woman: (*clutching the urn protectively*) I don't want my uncle turned into sneezing powder!
>
> Undertaker: Ah, very funny Modom. I'm afraid the ashes of deceased persons would never meet the required standard for sneezing powder. We merely place the ashes in the Garden of Remembrance.
>
> Woman: No tricks? No jokes?
>
> Undertaker: Indeed, no. Unless you count… but it is a very small one.
>
> Woman: A very small what?
>
> Undertaker: A very small rollercoaster – like the rest of the rides. Of course, we do have rather a large Haunted House.
>
> Woman: More a Funfair of Remembrance, really. I don't think my uncle would have wanted that.
>
> Undertaker: Was the deceased a little lacking in humour, perhaps?
>
> Woman: You can say that again. He was a traffic warden, very zealous. Even gave me a ticket once!
>
> Undertaker: Dear, dear.
>
> Woman: I was picking my aunt up from the doctor's. His wife! She was on crutches at the time. And I was only giving her a lift because he was too mean to pay for a taxi.
>
> (*They both stare at the urn.*)
>
> Woman: Bastard.
>
> Undertaker: Ex-bastard.

Woman: He didn't like Norman Wisdom, you know. Well, he didn't like any of them. Couldn't take a joke. He would have hated that funeral. Hated it. (*She smiles.*)

Undertaker: Modom is feeling better?

Woman: Oh, yes. Yes, indeed.

(*She laughs. The undertaker looks smug.*)

Finish the first draft

Now you're going to finish the first draft of your sketch:

1   Write the main body of your sketch.
2   Write the end of your sketch.

Key idea

If you're submitting work to an existing sketch show, stick with what you know the performers can do. Only established writers get to push the boundaries.

Editing

Once you've drafted the sketch, it's time to edit and polish. And guess what, the skills you've already practised when you were editing your jokes will also be useful with sketches. You still need to be economical with words, to be specific, to keep the best till last and so on. Oh, and as with jokes, don't throw away anything you have written – add the rejected material to your Spare Jokes folder.

Look at every speech and see whether you can do without it. I think 'Funeral Fun' can manage without this exchange:

Woman: ...She couldn't come. She's a bit upset, you see.

Undertaker: Quite understandable. The grieving widow.

Woman: Not about that. Well, naturally she is upset about that, we all are, and then there was the funeral, that was quite distressing, and then when the bill came it was the last straw.

Taking this out means that we get into the main part of the sketch much more quickly.

Next, go through each speech and check that it is economical with words while still being in character. For instance, 'Funeral Fun' can lose this 'A little obvious, perhaps, but most effective for a certain class of person.' It does add to the character of the undertaker, but it isn't essential. Don't leave in lines that are funny but irrelevant. It's tough but you have to take them out.

Now go through the sketch and mark where you think the laughs will be. Are there any that are too close together? Or any long gaps without a laugh? Check that nothing crucial is said or done immediately after a laugh.

Finally, have a good look at the ending. Does it fit the premise? If it doesn't and it goes off at a surreal tangent, are you sure the audience will be able to follow? As with most sketch drafts, the ending of 'Funeral Fun' does seem a little weak. The focus is on the uncle. His personality hasn't been described earlier in the sketch, and the fact that he was a thoroughly unpleasant man only appears at the end, which means that the sketch has gone off at a tangent. The question is, is that funny enough for the ending? How about ending the sketch when the boxing glove pops out of the urn? This keeps to the premise of the sketch, which is about mixing comedy with funerals. On the other hand, it means losing a speech that potentially has quite a lot of laughs in it:

> Woman: I was picking my aunt up from the doctor's. *Laugh* His wife! *Laugh* She was on crutches at the time. *Laugh* And I was only giving her a lift because he was too mean to pay for a taxi. *Laugh*.

So maybe the place to end the sketch is on the line 'Ex-bastard', which has a nice echo of 'ex-parrot'. It moves away from the premise, but it does mean that it ends on a twist. So, which ending to go for? I'm not sure – what do you think?

 ## Edit the detail of your sketch

1 Edit your sketch.
2 Mark the laughs.
3 Fine-tune the ending.

Where to next?

The simple characters that work so well in sketches won't be sustainable in a longer piece, so now we're going to look at creating more complex characters.

9

Creating more complex characters

So far we've looked at how to create the simple characters needed for stand-up, quickies, sketches and cartoons. For longer formats such as sitcoms, novels, plays and movies, the characters need to be more complex and developed – but still crisply conceived.

In this type of comedy, characters are more complex but are still fixed, with the laughs coming from what happens around them and their reactions to situations. Stock characters and stereotypes are no longer useful – except perhaps in bit parts – and characters now need to be highly individual. (Some longer comedies take characters to a different level altogether, which we'll look at in Chapter 12.)

In this chapter you will learn how to develop more fully rounded characters with motivations, desires and flaws, and how to put contrasting characters in the same piece for the best comic effect.

Focus point

Over the next few chapters you will create characters, a situation and a plot for a short piece. It can be a sitcom episode, a short story or a one-act play – it's your choice.

Ray Cooney, playwright

'If I had to give just one piece of comedy writing advice it would be: make it real.'

The elements of character

As with the shorter formats, the most important thing is to give your characters some sort of conflict. Characters need to be flawed in some way, and the flaw will arise from their inner conflict. Many comedy characters have flaws that the rest of us understand only too well, which is why we feel a connection with them. We can see our own failings reflected back to us. At the same time, one of the reasons we laugh at their misfortune, rather than commiserate, is that we can see they only have themselves to blame. So Father Ted is a lazy priest who can't be trusted with money, and Dave Lister (*Red Dwarf*) is a slob who never does anything properly.

Most successful comedy characters – such as Bertie Wooster, Del Boy (*Only Fools and Horses*) and Geraldine (*The Vicar of Dibley*) – are basically likeable, despite their failings. And there are other characters that we like because they get away with the things we would secretly love to do ourselves – Bernard Black in *Black Books* is rude to customers and shuts his shop whenever he feels like it, but he is still a likeable character.

However, there is a separate category of deeply unlikeable and unredeemed characters who are still comedically successful. We don't feel a connection with characters like Alan Partridge and David Brent (*The Office*), but the chances are that we know someone like them. In real life they can almost impossible to deal with – thick-skinned, self-centred, deluded – so it is amusing and satisfying to see how their fictional counterparts dig themselves ever deeper into a bottomless pit.

Finally, there is a small number of characters who are practically psychopathic, such as Jill Tyrell in *Nighty Night*. Inevitably the comedy is very dark, with as much pain as laughter, while we watch them ruin the lives of the innocent people around them and give thanks that we've never been the victim of someone like that.

> ## Key idea
>
> Conflict is still the most important requirement, but now you need to create characters that are more fully rounded.

Creating characters

The simplest way to achieve rounded individual characters is to write a biography for each one so that you get to know them in depth. The longer you make each biography the better you'll get to know your characters. Give each character a dominant trait or quirk and make them larger than life. The degree to which you do this will be part of what sets the tone for the comedy.

> ## Key idea
>
> Most of this knowledge won't find its way into the finished work, but it will inform and underpin your writing.

Here are some examples of short biographies:

- *Adam, 35, sees himself as a high-flying executive but actually he has a merchandising business putting company logos on T-shirts, mugs and biros. He still lives with his mum.*
- *Alex, 40, drives only the best cars, wears only the best suits and visits the most exclusive gyms. He works in finance, so he doesn't get up in the morning for less than 10k and he believes that money is there for spending.*
- *Colin, 55, is a middle-aged chauvinist with a beer gut and a strong conviction that women can't resist him. He considers himself the dominant male of any group. As far as he's concerned, women don't count – he doesn't know that the one thing they all agree on is that Colin is disgusting.*
- *Danyella, 16, is at that awkward age – it started when she was born and shows no sign of fading 16 years on. Her deepest relationship is with her mobile phone and she hates everyone older than 18.*

- *Laura, 47, runs The House of Relaxation, a centre for massage, reflexology, aromatherapy, etc. She talks about auras and spirit healing but only half-believes it all.*
- *Maisie, 53, is a middle-aged, overweight party girl and born survivor. She sleeps all day and goes clubbing at night. Her only worry in life is wondering where she left her knickers.*
- *Norman, 26 going on 50, is super-geeky, with a passion for counting things. He's never had a friend. In any group he wants to show off his knowledge but is always distracted by the need to check that everyone has a working biro.*
- *Stephanie, 28, doesn't mind being a fat girl, because it means she can give people even better hugs, like a sort of primitive earth mother but with more sensitivity due to her reading of self-help books. She knows that anger is just love turned inside out, so the more people shout at her the more she hugs them.*
- *Stuart, 30, is a naïve and insecure New Age type who lives off lentils and makes every sentence sound like a question.*
- *Wendy, 25, is a cynical young woman with a jaundiced view of the world. She has a computer science degree but finds it hard to get a job because of her chippy attitude.*

 Create biographies

Write short biographies for ten comedy characters. You can take them from your existing lists or create new ones.

 Focus point

If you're working with several characters, keep a file on each one, adding to it as you write to make sure you don't contradict yourself.

BACKGROUND AND BACKSTORY

You need to understand where each character comes from and how they reached the point they're at when the story starts. Are they, for instance, upwardly mobile or are they still living in the house where they were born? Did they have a happy or an unhappy childhood? Did they do well or badly at school? Wherever they are, think about how they got there, and why – there's a big difference between someone who is driven and someone who sits back and lets things happen.

- **Adam** – *ordinary family background, not very successful at school, although he did learn to talk his way out of trouble, usually by telling lies based on his inner fantasies.*
- **Alex** – *public-school educated but not academic. The men in his family are either solicitors or doctors, so he constantly needs to prove that finance is just as important and difficult.*
- **Colin** – *married his childhood sweetheart, who divorced him when she discovered feminism, leaving him with a massive chip, possibly on his shoulder, possibly elsewhere.*
- **Danyella** – *lives with her mum, her mum's boyfriend and several small children who are variously related to her and to each other. Spends a lot of time round her Nan's.*
- **Laura** – *like many twins, she's determined to be different from her twin sister Angela. Since Angela is married to a high-flying executive type with the lifestyle to match, Laura has gone the other way. Her gap year lasted a decade as she pursued an interest in alternative lifestyles. She doesn't have much money as a result, and is secretly jealous of her sister's big house, smart cars and fancy holidays.*
- **Maisie** – *used to work in a sweet factory before it closed; famously the only employee who never got tired of sampling the product. Has definitely been married and has children, but is vague about the details.*
- **Norman** – *brought up by his doting mother after his dad left home following a row about the correct way to serve smoked salmon. She taught him that it was never possible to be too tidy.*
- **Stephanie** – *the oldest of a large family, she likes to be the mother figure as it's all she knows.*
- **Stuart** – *both his parents were hippies living in a commune in the 1960s, and when that broke down they never really adjusted to the real world, where they are both teachers.*
- **Wendy** – *an only child. Her middle-class aspirational mother was very competitive in all Wendy's activities, apart from social skills.*

Create backgrounds

Create brief backgrounds for your ten characters.

MOTIVATION, DOMINANT DESIRE AND FLAWS

We all have things that we think we ought to be doing ('I really ought to lose ten pounds', 'I really ought to clean the car') but, unless those things somehow connect with our deep motivation in life, we probably won't get round to doing them. If your character's key motivation is vanity, they will probably lose the weight while driving round in a filthy car, whereas the reverse might be true of someone whose key motivation was to maintain their social standing.

 Key idea

Successful comedy characters need an obvious and simple key motivation that audiences can identify with.

Comedy is full of odd, quirky and eccentric characters whose motivation is usually on the surface for everyone to see. *The Vicar of Dibley* is packed to the church rafters with eccentrics but every one is clearly drawn, with easily understood motivation: David Horton needs to be in charge; over-sexed Owen Newitt ignores the conventions of polite society; Letitia Cropley loves to cook but has no sense of taste, and so on. However, we all have deeper drives that are less obvious, even to ourselves, and the same is true of comedy characters. Why is the vain character vain? Is it because he or she was a plain child, and constantly teased about their appearance? Or is it the opposite – that they were good-looking when young and are determined to hang on to the kudos that this brings them?

When you're creating characters, they will be much more real if you work out what their deep motivation is, but you don't have to reveal this to the audience, and the character doesn't have to be aware of it. In *The Vicar of Dibley*, we do gain insight into downtrodden Hugo Horton because we meet his father, but the other characters mainly keep their secrets. In fact, keeping that knowledge to yourself can make a character more realistic, since very few people are aware of their deep motivation (unless, of course, they've had years of expensive therapy).

A character's dominant desire arises out of their motivation and their reaction to their life situation. David Horton needs to be in charge of the Parish Council, but he could just as well be an office manager or an Army officer – the motivation and desire to run things would be the same.

Key idea

Some writers think that keeping their characters' core secrets is the key to success.

Lesley Bown, writer

'The first draft of my novel Going Through the Motions had a lot about the main character's childhood (her father was a ladies' hairdresser, her mother drove a London bus), but in the second draft I took it all out – it was enough for me to know how her character was formed.'

While some elements of a character's motivation and dominant desire will be explained by their background and backstory, don't forget that some people's characteristics are often inexplicable – some people are just born that way and everyone is flawed to some extent.

- *Adam wants other people to be impressed by his material success but hasn't got the talent to be successful. Lazy.*
- *Alex is only interested in money and has no spiritual depth. Greedy.*
- *Colin still lives by outdated macho beliefs and has no self-insight. Bullying.*
- *Danyella lives in the moment with no thought for tomorrow. Self-centred.*
- *Laura is drawn to the world of alternative therapies because she likes the hippy image but doesn't really believe in any of it. Manipulative.*
- *Maisie just wants to have a good time and never got round to growing up. Thoughtless.*
- *Norman wants to organize the world and has no empathy for other people. Over-intense.*
- *Stephanie is terrified of looking inside herself, so focuses on caring for other people. Greedy.*
- *Stuart is unable to engage with harsh reality. Impractical.*
- *Wendy wants to impress people with her cleverness. Rude.*

Flesh out your characters

For each of your characters, work out their motivation, their dominant desire and their main flaw.

THE UNSEEN CHARACTER

The unseen character in a piece can be a useful source of comedy, because it can be far more extreme than a character we see. Of course they can only ever be a minor character but they can add another layer of comedy. You can see the different effects of this in the sitcom *The Good Life*, where we never meet the two characters that plague Margo Leadbetter: Miss Mountshaft of the Music Society and Mrs Dooms-Paterson of the Pony Club. We do, however, meet Sir, Tom's ex-boss and Jerry's current boss, in some episodes. Sir is set up as a megalomaniac and a heartless boss, but inevitably he seems a little too human when we meet him. The two unseen characters are far more extreme.

Key idea

You should develop the unseen character fully, and take particular care to understand the dominant desire that causes them to behave as they do, and the nature of the relationship with the seen character.

Selecting characters

Looking down your lists, which characters are you drawn to? We all have our own preferences, and as writers we'll create and work with characters that speak to us in some way.

For the lists above, I wouldn't want to write about Alex but I could do something with Adam. Equally, I wouldn't pick Stephanie because I don't see anything funny in weight issues, but I can see plenty of comedy potential in two-faced Laura. Another writer might be able to make something out of Alex and Stephanie.

Assess comedy potential

Assess your characters for their comedy potential and decide which ones appeal to you as a writer.

SUBTEXT AND AGENDAS

There is always more to a character than meets the eye. You may be talking to someone perfectly cheerfully but thinking about something else the whole time – how boring they are, what you fancy for your dinner, whether the gas bill is due yet and so on. For storytelling purposes, these things need to be conveyed to the audience.

The broad spectrum of hidden meanings is known as subtext. Agendas are rather more specific. Someone has an agenda when they go into a situation knowing what they want to get out of it. We all do it, and it has great comedy potential. For instance, a man wants to get to a football match but his partner insists that he help her choose new cushions. As long as his love of football has been set up in advance, there are a lot of laughs to be gained from the way he will want to buy the first cushions they see, suitably hideous of course, and will pay through the nose for them. Then, when his partner tells him to take them home with him, naturally he'll take them to the football match instead, and they'll get damaged in some way, or he'll lose them and have to find others.

Subtext and agendas are not the same as internal conflict. A character's internal conflict doesn't change, whereas subtext and agendas change according to the situation. However, a character's dominant desire will usually be the driving force behind their agenda in any given situation.

BODY LANGUAGE

Apparently we reveal more about our thoughts through body language than through what we say. For instance, someone scratching their neck is supposed to be doubting the truth of what they're hearing. A character like No Offence, the beauty adviser in *The Fast Show*, has obsequious body language while making offensive remarks, which adds to the comedy. In the same show, the body language of Ted and Ralph is what tells us there is something going on under the surface of the master/servant relationship.

VOICE

Consider how your character speaks – Received Pronunciation or strong regional accent? Which region? When you're thinking about this, remember that English audiences have ingrained presumptions about accents. Scots are canny, Londoners are fly, country people are slow and so on. When you're writing jokes, quickies and sketches you can make use of these stock qualities, but otherwise use them only if they absolutely meet your writing needs.

When you first start writing, you may find that you choose voices based on your own favourite fictional characters. Once you've corrected that habit, you might tend to give all your characters your own voice. And once you've corrected that habit, you can get down to giving characters their own, unique voice.

VOCABULARY

In the first draft of a piece you'll just be concerned about getting the words down so that you can reach the end of the draft, but part of the polishing process is to make sure that each character has an appropriate vocabulary and uses it consistently. Decide whether they use slang or jargon and, if they do, decide whether they are up to date or a bit behind the times.

SPEECH PATTERNS

Think about a character's speech pattern – do they talk fast in quick sentences or have a slow, ponderous delivery? I hear these voices for my characters – you may hear others:

- **Adam** *uses slang and jargon that are out of date.*
- **Alex** *has a public-school accent and uses jargon to baffle listeners.*
- **Colin** *has an Essex accent and talks tough.*
- **Danyella** *uses teenage street talk, when she does talk – mainly she texts.*
- **Laura** *softly spoken and has all the hippy-dippy vocabulary at the tip of her tongue.*
- **Maisie** *has a Leeds accent and calls a spade a ****ing spade.*
- **Norman** *hesitates a lot because he's trying to be precise.*
- **Stephanie** *chatters incessantly and has a loud laugh.*
- **Stuart** *treats every sentence like a question and is very politically correct.*
- **Wendy** *sharp-tongued, cynical and sarcastic.*

How do your characters speak?

Think about voice, vocabulary and speech pattern for your characters.

NAMES

Naming a character is part of bringing it to life and can also tell the audience a lot about a character. Think about the probable differences between say, a Tarquin and a Derek. If you choose a funny name for your character, you'll be consigning it to the cartoonish, one-dimensional end of the spectrum – not necessarily a bad thing, of course. Names can also give the audience a clue to the nature of the character – Fawlty, for instance, is clearly Faulty. When you're choosing names, think also about diminutives and pet names.

> ## Simon Brett, writer
>
> *'Don't agonize over thinking of funny lines. If you've got the relationship between the characters right, the lines will come out funny.'*

Characters combined

Once your characters are individually formed, you have to start putting them together. Contrasting characters give more opportunities for comedy, and a lot of comedy comes from conflict between characters. Aim for a balance between eccentric characters and relatively normal ones. For instance, in the TV series *Coupling* the characters of Jane and Jeff are more eccentric than the other four characters, which creates balance. Eccentric people are often unaware that their behaviour is extreme, and so the reactions of the more normal characters both underline the eccentricity and create laughs.

Looking down my list of characters, I like the look of Laura with either Alex or Adam as a mismatched pair who would have plenty of conflict, or maybe Norman and Maisie. Drippy Stuart with cold-hearted Wendy is another possibility, although Wendy would also struggle to get along with Danyella. Alex and Stephanie would have endless conflict, as would Norman and Colin.

BINDING TIES

Whatever type of situation you're putting them in, there is one big question you'll need to answer. Why do they stand for it? If they annoy each other so much, drive each other up the wall and round the bend, why don't they just get out and away from each other? The answer is in the binding ties that keep people together despite the conflict between them.

Focus point

Binding ties are the emotional connections that keep us with people who drive us mad: we love our annoying teenage children too much to kick them out of the house; we enjoy the income produced by the job that frustrates us so much; and we like the social status of living in the exclusive road full of mind-bendingly dull people.

Understanding binding ties requires deep psychological insight, although you don't need to know the jargon. Words like co-dependency and symbiosis are used to describe unhealthy relationships, but they simply mean that people can be simultaneously unable to get on with each other and yet need each other too. For instance, the two characters in *Steptoe and Son* are always at each other's throats but they still stay together. The audience is made aware that, despite all his bluster and social ambitions, the son does actually need the father and would struggle without him.

Binding ties are one of the staples of comedy writing but they to be very subtly done – too much and the whole thing turns schmaltzy, too little and the audience won't believe in the relationships.

Key idea

Binding ties are particularly important in sitcoms, because characters stay together week after week, and this needs to be believable. As long as the ties are strong enough, the audience will accept the situation. Of course, practical considerations are part of what keeps people together and those arise out of the situation they find themselves in (see Chapter 10 for more on this). The hardest ties to write well are the purely emotional ones – in *Keeping up Appearances* it is hard to know why the husband and sisters of the dreadful Hyacinth Bucket put up with her, apart from the emotional ties.

For comedy purposes, characters who have binding ties with each other should want different things from life, in order to create conflict. I'd pair my characters like this:

- *Adam and Laura could be brother and sister or business contacts.*
- *Alex and Maisie could be co-workers, with Maisie the cleaner in Alex's office.*
- *Colin and Norman could be neighbours.*
- *Danyella and Stephanie could be student and school counsellor.*
- *Stuart and Wendy are unlikely to be boyfriend and girlfriend but could be siblings or co-workers.*

Workshop

Now you've got to know your characters, it's time to put them together. Start with pairs to keep things simple. Decide which characters from your list would have comedy conflict. Examine where the conflict arises:

- Are they interested in similar things but have contrasting personalities?
- Are they from different parts of the social spectrum?
- Do they want different things from life?

Once you've got five nicely conflicted pairs, decide how they might be forced to interact – in other words, their binding ties.

- Are they family members?
- Are they neighbours?
- Are they work colleagues?
- Is it something else, such as being marooned on a desert island?

DIALOGUE

Dialogue between characters is multi-functional. It conveys character, moves the plot forward and gives information. If you're writing for performance, dialogue will be your main means of communication with an audience, whereas prose writers have the luxury of being able to describe a character's inner workings.

Drafting out sample dialogue is the quickest way to get to know how your characters interact with each other. Early drafts don't have to be funny – they are part of the learning process – but you do need to get a feeling for where the comedy might come from.

Laura: (chanting) *Ohmmmm...*

Adam: *Good, great, lovely. Now I just had this idea...*

Laura: *Ohmmmm...*

Adam: *Just thought I'd run it up the flagpole and see how it fluttered...*

Laura: *Ohmmmm...*

Adam: *You see, what you need here is some marketing input. This room, for instance...*

Laura: *There's nothing wrong with this room.*

Adam: *Wasted space. If you split it into two rooms, you could rent one of them out and double your income.*

Laura: *I couldn't possibly. I need the space. I need to feel emptiness round me when I meditate.*

Adam: *Then there's the sound system. What's this we're listening to, for instance?*

Laura: *Temple Bells. Very soothing.*

Adam: *Yes. But does it put people in the mood for spending? Will they go out of here primed and ready to choose from your display of organic relaxation products placed strategically next to the credit card facility?*

Laura: *We haven't got a display of relaxation products. Or a credit card facility.*

Adam: *No, but you will have, you will have.*

Write some dialogue

Write some sample dialogue for two of your characters that are in conflict. Don't struggle to make it funny at this stage – just write and see what happens. You already understand how they know each other, so use that situation for the dialogue. (If you like, repeat this exercise for the other four pairs.)

Subtext can also be conveyed through speech, for instance via the Freudian slip. There are all sorts of explanations for this tendency to say one thing when you mean another, but for comedy purposes we assume that the one that suggests it arises from what you're really thinking but would rather hide.

Another technique is to have a character express strong negative views about something that are clearly not true. A subtle variation of this is when a character appears to be talking about a third person but it becomes clear that they are actually talking about themselves.

SOMEONE TO CONFIDE IN

If you're writing for performance, you're likely to find that your main character needs a sidekick, someone to share things with and someone who helps them out. There will still be some conflict, no doubt, but basically they will be on the same side. For performance, this is one of the best ways of conveying the detail of a character's thoughts. Prose writers, of course, can dive straight in and tell their readers, but the sidekick is still useful because it avoids the need for too much description of a character's inner thoughts, which can send a reader off to sleep.

I could arrange sidekicks like this:

- *Adam and Wendy: both lack social skills so have no other friends.*
- *Alex and Norman: Alex is a show-off and Norman would admire him.*
- *Colin and Stephanie: Stephanie is too soft-hearted to tell Colin to push off.*
- *Danyella and Maisie share the same interests.*
- *Laura and Stuart are two of a kind.*

These all look reasonable, apart from Colin and Stephanie, which isn't a natural pairing: Colin would want a mate to watch football with and Stephanie would be more likely to latch on to Norman. I'd need to create new sidekicks for those two.

Although there is conflict in the relationship at the same time there is friendship, or something close to it. In the sitcom *Miranda*, Miranda confides in her friend Stevie while at the same time she is often pretty horrid to her. The fact that they work together provides a binding tie.

Again, it's a good idea to draft out some dialogue so you can learn how the characters interact.

Stuart: *The thing about people dying, Laura, it's just like, so so stressful?*

Laura: *Yes. Yes it is. Let's breathe the stress away, Stuart. Take in a breath, then let it out slowly. Slowly. Slooooowly.*

Stuart: *It's no good, I can't do it.*

Laura: *Stuart, just...*

Stuart: It's like, the appointment book? All these pages set aside for Margaret? What can I do with them, Laura? What can I do?

Laura: Well, er, take them out and...

Stuart: Yes! I will! I will take them out and I'll put them with Margaret's candle. That way, we can still remember her, but I won't be haunted by her empty pages in the appointment book.

Laura: Yes. Life is a mystery, don't you think?

Stuart: Oh yes. Laura...

Laura: And death. Death is a mystery, too.

Stuart: Yes. Laura, you know the appointment book is empty? I mean your side? Your side of the book is empty for today. And tomorrow.

Laura: Margaret did say a tree, didn't she?

Stuart: And next week.

Laura: Definitely coming back as a tree?

Stuart: Yes. A silver birch. A lovely, floppy one.

Laura: It's just that they are rather large.

Stuart: We could plant her outside.

Laura: Ah, she'd be lonely outside.

Stuart: Oh, no. She'd like to see the sun. And the moon.

Make friends

Rearrange your characters into pairs with less conflict and therefore more chance of being friends. Looking at the dialogue you've already written, choose one of those two characters, add their sidekick and write another short dialogue between the two.

Where to next?

Longer comedy formats need not only more complicated characters, they also need more complicated plots and subplots. The next chapter examines plotting in detail.

10

More complex situations and plots

As well as strong, funny characters, longer forms of comedy need to include more complex situations and a plot. This can be anything from a tightly crafted traditional farce to the much looser requirements of a diary-format novel. In comedy writing, plots are often circular, returning characters to the place they started out from. This is especially true of sitcoms.

In this chapter you will learn about the key elements of plotting and how to construct an effective story arc with a satisfying ending.

Do plots have to be funny?

Here's an example of a comedy plot:

> A man's annoying behaviour drives his wife to the point of divorce. When she throws him out, he decides to kill himself, so his best friend takes him in. He gradually annoys his friend so much that *he* throws him out, but immediately regrets it in case it prompts another suicide attempt. After searching the city for his friend, he finally finds him staying with some neighbours. They make their peace with each other and their friendship is saved.

Not a lot of laughs in that, perhaps – except that it's the plot of *The Odd Couple*, one of the all-time great comedy movies. So clearly a comedy plot doesn't have to be amusing in itself. Here's another example:

> Two musicians witness a gangland killing and go into hiding disguised as women. They join an all-female band. One of them is attracted to a beautiful fellow band member and in order to woo her he changes back into men's clothes and pretends to be a millionaire. He has constant costume changes and is often nearly caught out. The other one is pursued by a real millionaire, who is fooled by his disguise and proposes marriage. Everything is complicated by the fact that the gangsters are staying in the same hotel. In the end the musicians escape from the gangsters and both come clean about their disguises. Both the beautiful fellow band member and, surprisingly, the millionaire, are happy about this.

Yes, that's right, it's *Some Like It Hot*, another all-time great comedy movie, and one with a very funny plot.

So it's not necessary for your plot to be funny in itself, but if it is you'll start ahead of the game in terms of getting laughs. You can also see that the plot of *Some Like It Hot* is far more complicated than the plot of *The Odd Couple*.

Conflict and claustrophobia

For all forms of creative writing, the situation you choose for your characters is absolutely critical. It needs to provide two elements: conflict and claustrophobia. We've already looked at the three different types of conflict a character can experience (internal, interpersonal and societal) and clearly the situation you place them in can rack up the conflict.

Let's carry on working with the characters from Chapter 9:

The dialogue between Adam and Laura shows him trying to sell her his services, which she doesn't really want. If they are related to each other, she might find it difficult to turn him down but since her character is quite devious she'd probably find a way. On the other hand, if they worked together there would be conflict because of their differing agendas, or they could be neighbours, perhaps.

Situations that increase conflict

Take your five character pairs from Chapter 9. You already know what their binding ties are, but now create situations that will increase their conflict.

Claustrophobia in this context simply means placing characters in situations they can't escape from, so that they have to find a way of rubbing along together. Binding ties are what make people stay together for emotional and psychological reasons. Claustrophobic situations force them together for practical reasons: changing jobs is not always an option, divorce is expensive, elderly parents need looking after and so on.

In *Steptoe and Son*, the ties are both emotional (because they are father and son) and practical (because they run a business together). In *Porridge*, the ties are entirely practical – the characters are in prison and have no choice about staying together.

Red Dwarf took this to the ultimate extreme by marooning the characters in a spaceship. This definitely increased the conflict between the characters, but you can see the potential problem for a sitcom writer who needs to keep coming up with plots – the more isolated a group of characters are, the harder it is to think up new things that could happen to them. The writers of *Red Dwarf* needed to constantly engineer encounters with other spaceships, alien civilizations and so on.

Jane Austen was fully aware of the principle of claustrophobia when she wrote that for an author 'three or four families in a country village is the very thing to work on'. In the eighteenth century people were not as socially mobile as they are now, and so families tended to stay put in their home village. This gave her two levels of claustrophobia – within the family and within the small society of a village.

If Adam and Laura were working in the same office there would have to be good reasons why neither of them could leave, which would increase the claustrophobia. They probably wouldn't choose to share premises, so this situation would need to be forced on them in some way.

Check for claustrophobia

Check your situations for claustrophobia: ask how easy it would be for the characters to walk away.

Ann Gawthorpe, writer

'If I had to give just one piece of comedy writing advice, it would be: know when to give the audience/reader prior information to create comedy – and when not to.'

Creating a story

Conflicted characters and a claustrophobic situation aren't enough. You also need a story, or plot. Sometimes it will be obvious from the characters and their situation what the story should be, but sometimes you'll have to start from scratch.

Key idea

Of course, every type of story has already been told but, equally, every old story can be reinterpreted and given a new twist.

Here are some basic story ideas:

- **The quest.** This is one of the oldest story forms. A character sets out on a quest to find something and has adventures along the way. It doesn't have to be a physical journey – the quest can be for anything from a Golden Fleece to inner peace. Most stories, in fact, can be interpreted as quests.

- **Love.** Finding it, losing it and the complications associated with it. Recently, Richard Curtis has been the king of love-based comedy, with his films *Four Weddings and a Funeral*, *Notting Hill* and *Love Actually*.

- **Hate.** The trigger is something that causes the characters to fall out and the story is about how the argument escalates and is resolved. The Christmas TV drama *Christmas Lights* used the concept of two men falling out over who could create the most spectacular Christmas display, and it was so successful that it lead to two series and a second Christmas special.

- **Accident.** Stories based round accidents can give rise to a lot of physical comedy, for instance as a character struggles to go through their normal life with an arm or a leg in plaster.

- **Sudden riches or poverty.** Either situation produces great comedy. Sue Townsend sent the Queen to live on a council estate in *The Queen and I*, whereas *The Beverly Hillbillies* is about a poor family who strike it rich.

- **An outsider.** Any new person introduced into a stable set-up can cause comedy mayhem. An elderly parent moving in with their children and grandchildren, a new boss at work, or someone retiring and being at home instead of at work.

- **Special occasions.** Weddings, Christmas, and other big life events can all make for good stories. A funeral can make a good plot trigger and divorce has proved to be fertile ground for sitcoms (*My Wife Next Door, Home To Roost, Teenage Kicks*) and movies (*Mrs Doubtfire, Liar Liar*).

- **Something to hide.** A protagonist with something to hide is a staple of traditional farce – in *Charley's Aunt* a man tries to pass himself off as the Aunt and he clearly has something to hide. It is also found in many other types of comedy.

- **Misunderstandings.** This is another staple of farce that can be used in many ways. For instance, an early episode of *Men Behaving Badly* had Gary form a mistaken impression that his new flatmate Tony was gay.

- **Incompetence.** For many characters this would come under 'something to hide', but not always – for instance, Frank Spencer in the classic sitcom *Some Mothers Do 'Ave 'Em* is openly useless.
- **The fish out of water, or role reversal.** Any story that places a character in an unfamiliar environment has comedy potential.
- **Moral or ethical issues.** This may not seem like the stuff of comedy, but many plots hang on a moral dilemma. The US series *My Name is Earl* is entirely about a small-time criminal who is trying to cancel out his bad past by doing good deeds.

Roughing out a plot

Once you have a situation and an idea of what sort of plot you want to create, it's time to start asking 'What if?' Let your answers be as far-fetched as possible. For each answer, ask 'What next?' Keep doing this until you find a sequence of events that will give you a plot. Choose the answers that walk the fine line between believable and ridiculous, and above all the ones that have the best comedy potential.

Adam and Laura have to work together in the same office. Adam is a marketing consultant; Laura does alternative therapies. The two businesses are not compatible. What if there was a mix-up in Reception and each of them saw the wrong client? How would a businessman feel about being asked to relax and smell the roses? How would a New Age type feel about being given a marketing talk? Would they both storm out and refuse to pay? What if they both liked it and it changed their lives?

Ask questions

Choose the character pair that seems to you to have the most comedy potential, which means the most conflict, the strongest binding ties and the most claustrophobic situation. Ask 'What if?' and 'What next?' Keep going until you feel able to rough out a plot for a one-act play or short story. (We'll look at sitcoms in the next chapter.)

Chris Ritchie, creator of
the innovative Comedy:
Writing & Performance degree
at Southampton Solent University
and editor of *Comedy Studies*

'Be honest. Talk about what is real to you, what is believable.
If an audience finds something funny as well as interesting,
if they learn something, then the performance is going to be
more memorable. Tell us something we don't know!'

BACKSTORY, TRIGGER AND EXPOSITION

The backstory is everything that has happened to the characters
up until the moment the story starts. Some of this will be revealed;
some will remain hidden. The simpler the situation, the more quickly
and easily an audience connects with it, which is why plots about
family life, office life, neighbourhood life and so on are so popular.

The trigger is the incident that sets the story in motion. Jane Austen
understood that every story needs a trigger. In *Pride and Prejudice*,
for instance, the trigger is the arrival of an eligible and wealthy
young bachelor in the village.

In order to understand the significance of the trigger, the audience
needs a certain amount of explanation about the characters and their
situation. This is known as exposition. The challenge for the writer is
to give all the information in a way that isn't too obvious or boring.
Pride and Prejudice provides a masterclass in how to do this. In the first
300 words we learn that eligible Mr Bingley has moved to the area,
that the Bennets have unmarried daughters, that Mrs Bennet wants to
marry them off, and that Mr Bennet maintains a position of humorous
detachment. We also as a result have a pretty good idea of the character
of both Mr and Mrs Bennet and the way their marriage works, or
doesn't work, and we've been both amused and sucked into the story.

Starting the story at the moment of the trigger ensures that the plot
will engage the audience immediately, but it's not the only way to do
it. The opening scene of the movie *Men in Black* is nine minutes long,
and only reaches the trigger at the end of the scene, when Agent D
decides to retire. The scene is a well-crafted little story that sets the
tone for the whole movie, with its mixture of comedy and drama. Of
all the characters in the long opening sequence, only Agent K is seen
again, but much information has been conveyed and the audience has
been put into the right frame of mind for the rest of the movie.

The exposition for *Men in Black* is particularly challenging as it describes an original set-up that requires lengthy explanation. (In case you haven't seen the movie, it is about an American agency that oversees the aliens who live, for the most part, peacefully among us and about which the rest of us know nothing.) The agency isn't mentioned at all until 17 minutes into the movie, and the full explanation comes 28 minutes in when a new agent is recruited. By then, of course, the audience should be hooked and willing to sit through a few minutes of explanation.

The trigger will be the fact that Adam and Laura need to share premises, and the exposition will need to explain how and why this happened. It could be a complicated legal thing or a simple money-saving exercise for both of them, but there is not a lot of comedy potential there. What if there was a misunderstanding? That would need a lot of exposition. In fact, it would be enough on its own to fill a short piece. Perhaps they could be family, so that one of them felt obliged to let the other one share the office. Perhaps one of them could acquire a share of the other's premises, by inheritance maybe?

So, when Laura's business partner dies, it's discovered that she's left her share of The House of Relaxation to her nephew Adam. He isn't interested in relaxation, but he does want to use the premises for his own business. This means that Adam isn't related to Laura, so there are no ties of affection to soften their relationship. (This solution also means that I can make some use of the lists and jokes I generated for the 'Funeral Fun' sketch.)

Workshop

Think about the trigger for your plot:
- Will one of the characters do something that triggers the plot, such as deciding to leave home?
- Will the trigger be an external event, such as a lottery win?

Now decide how much exposition is needed. You will need to establish:
- the basics of each character
- their relationship and binding ties
- their situation
- the trigger.

As this is to be a short piece, choose the options that give you the least complicated exposition.

CRISES

Constructing a plot consists of taking your characters from the trigger, through a series of crises or obstacles, to a climax followed by a resolution. The crises need to be of increasing severity. It works particularly well if the solution of one crisis is the very thing that gives rise to the next crisis, so that the characters seem to be digging themselves ever deeper into a hole, and are ever closer to total meltdown. The final crisis produces the climax, and after that the plot should move swiftly to the resolution.

Focus point

This basic plot shape of a slow but steadily increasing build-up followed by a quick finale is known as a dramatic arc. It works for all types of writing and for all genres.

The crises will arise from the mix-up over clients. Perhaps there is only one phone line with clients phoning in for both businesses. Also there may be a shared appointment book, or two books that look identical. If there were two receptionists, one for each business, then Adam and Laura would each have a sidekick. Maybe, instead of two books, the New Age business would have an old-fashioned book but the marketing business would have an electronic system. Adam and Laura each see the wrong client.

Crises and obstacles

Re-examine your 'what ifs' and your rough sequence of events. Make sure there are plenty of crises and obstacles.

SUBPLOTS

A substantial piece of storytelling is unlikely to get by with just one plot. A subplot is a smaller story running alongside, and secondary to, the main plot. It can involve minor characters or be a series of incidents in the protagonist's life that are less important than the main plot. Of course, there can be more than one subplot. It's most satisfying if the subplots are resolved in ways that feed into the resolution of the main plot. This is expertly done in the movie *Little Miss Sunshine*. The main plot is about seven-year-old Olive's desire to enter a beauty pageant, but each of her five older relatives has a subplot.

One function of subplots is that they keep minor characters busy. P. G. Wodehouse said that writers should think of their characters as actors in a play: since they're being paid, they need to be on stage and not just sitting in a dressing room because they've said their one and only line.

The two receptionists are an obvious source of a subplot. They could be attracted to each other despite their differences, or they could argue constantly. The mix-up over clients would be their fault. They could fall out over how to arrange the reception area – will it be what Adam wants or what Laura wants? Another subplot could come from the story behind the inheritance – this would incorporate some of the exposition into the plot. The two clients could also have their own subplot.

Create a subplot

Devise a subplot using the two sidekicks from the exercise in Chapter 9. You don't need a separate trigger for the subplot, but otherwise work through the same steps as for your main plot.

1 Look at the ties that bind them to the main characters.
2 Look at the relationships between them.
3 Look at their situation: in what way they are part of the main plot?
4 Finally, look at how their plotline can run alongside the main plot.

ENDINGS

Endings are always important. Whatever you're writing, it will be the ending that stays with the audience, that creates catharsis or sets them thinking.

Many writers struggle with endings, perhaps because in life there are few complete endings – something always happens next. There are several types of ending and you need to make a clear choice:

- **Closed ending:** Here, just about everything is resolved, particularly in the story of the main characters. For instance, if you end with a wedding or a funeral then you have taken the story to a natural stopping point. The same is true if the characters are on a quest, in which they succeed at the end. With this type of ending the characters can never return to the point at which they started – things have changed irrevocably for them.

- **Circular ending:** The characters do return to the point at which they started. This type of ending is essential in sitcoms, where the characters and their situation must be the same every week. At the same time, you do have to resolve the immediate problem that you've set. So you could create a story where a husband and wife have a conflict – perhaps they can't decide where to go for their holiday. She wants a beach holiday; he wants an adventure holiday. This will have to be resolved by the end of the episode – by compromise, or by one of them winning the argument, perhaps – but the resolution can't lead to divorce or any other permanent change to the status quo.

- **Open ending:** An ending that doesn't resolve anything. This type of ending is the most difficult to achieve successfully, because audiences on the whole want to know how the story ends – hence the debate about the ending of the original version of *The Italian Job*, still going on after more than 40 years. However, in comedy there is more flexibility and open endings can be made to work well. In *The Goon Show* there were quite a few open endings – for instance, the episode titled 'The Dreaded Batter-Pudding Hurler (of Bexhill-on-Sea)' has two endings: first, listeners are invited to write in with suggestions for the ending and then there is a marriage proposal that has nothing to do with the plot.

HAPPY OR SAD?

It is not compulsory for a comedy to have a happy ending, although very few have a truly sad ending. The last episode of the sitcom *Blackadder* famously ends with the soldiers going over the top to fight, undoubtedly to be killed. It is extremely powerful and a rare example of a sad ending.

Most writers choose either a happy ending or a mixed ending. If the main character has been selfish, dishonest or has behaved badly in some other way, then there is a choice as to whether they get away with it at the end or get their comeuppance.

CONSTRUCTING AN ENDING

If you're constructing a closed or circular ending, then aim for something that is both logical and unexpected. In other words, the audience is unlikely to anticipate the ending but when it arrives it makes perfect sense. The surprise element should ensure that there is a big laugh at the end. Open endings also need to generate a laugh and be unexpected, but by definition aren't logical.

Writers are usually advised to avoid using '*deus ex machina*' or 'god in the machine' endings. This refers to a habit in ancient Greek drama of ending a story by having the gods intervene. Any kind of supernatural intervention or introduction of a new factor or character usually makes for an unsatisfying ending because it hasn't arisen out of the story.

However, in comedy, *deus ex machina* endings can work if they are appropriate to the type of comedy. In a conventional sitcom it wouldn't work if, for instance, the couple arguing about the holiday were suddenly given enough money to be able to afford both types of holiday. On the other hand, Monty Python sketches often ended with an unexpected and unexplained intervention, for instance from the Anti-Silliness Patrol.

This is a simple story that requires a conventional closed ending to the main plot. The big question is, will there be a winner and a loser, two winners or two losers? Anything is possible, but one ending might be that Adam is angry because he has seen the wrong client and lost the business, while Laura is smug because she was successful with her client even though it was the wrong one. Then they notice that the receptionists have rearranged the furniture the way Adam wanted. Now Laura is angry, while Adam is smug.

Look at the ending

You probably already have an idea how your main plot and subplot will end, but now revisit the ending and examine it in detail.

Jan Etherington, award-winning comedy writer, broadcaster and journalist

'*It's very hard for new comedy writers to hang on to their vision, their original idea, their words and their sanity, because many people will offer an opinion of your work and very little of it will be constructive, or even right. Comedy writers are not trusted to know what's funny, because everyone thinks they have funny bones. Keep your sense of humour – but keep a hit list!*'

Other types of plot

DIARIES AND LETTERS

One alternative to tightly controlled plotting is to use a looser, more episodic structure. This tends to work best for prose rather than performance, particularly in comedy diaries and letters.

There is a long history of comedy diaries, reaching back to *The Diary of a Nobody* published in 1888. Rather than a plot, diaries tend to have a series of running themes. For instance, in *The Timewaster Diaries* by Robin Cooper, the dominant theme is his passion for inventing the most bizarre things, and other themes include his wife constantly spraining her ankle and his Swiss penfriend's frequent puzzling references to 'house handles'. By the end of the year, it looks as if one of his inventions is about to pay off, which is enough of an ending to satisfy the reader.

A variation on the diary idea is letters, seen most recently in the radio comedy *Ladies of Letters*, which again is fairly loosely plotted.

LINKED STORIES

Another approach to plotting, much favoured by P. G. Wodehouse, is to write a series of linked short stories. The same central characters have a series of comic adventures rather like the episodes of a sitcom. And, like a sitcom, the individual stories have to be carefully plotted.

Other aspects of plot construction

THE RULE OF THREE

You've already seen that putting things in threes is a good comedy structure, and this extends to plot construction. The rule of three is important for conveying important information. If you can find ways to mention something three times, then you can be sure of getting it across, but do create variety in the ways it's mentioned and only do this for really important information.

SHOW DON'T TELL

This means that character should be revealed through action rather than exposition. It applies particularly to performance, although prose writers need to be aware of it, too, because too much explanation can make for heavy reading. If two characters don't get on, you can convey that information by having one of them say, 'I can't stand X', but it is much more effective to show the hostility between them through an event in the plot.

REINCORPORATION

You've already seen that reincorporation can work in stand-up routines, and it is also extremely valuable in plotting. Set something up early on, and then don't refer to it again until much later. It can be something that comes back to cause a problem for a character, or it can be used in the resolution.

As part of an ending, reincorporation is particularly effective. It creates an ending that is both surprising, because the audience has forgotten about whatever it is, and logical, because it was set up earlier. For example, about halfway through the *Absolutely Fabulous* episode 'New Best Friend', Eddy's visitors are seen setting up the baby alarm. Then the very last scene uses the alarm, which has been left switched on, to finish the story. The crucial thing is that there is no mention of the alarm at all once it's set up, so that the audience forgets about it.

IRONY

In plot terms, irony means that not everyone knows what is going on. Maybe the audience knows something that none of the characters knows, or maybe all the characters except one know something. *Friends* got a lot of mileage out of the romance between Chandler and Monica, which the other characters didn't know about but the audience did.

Case history: a plot analysed

Oscar Wilde's enduring comedy *The Importance of Being Earnest* was first performed in 1895 and is still regularly revived.

BACKSTORY

Jack Worthing was adopted by a wealthy man, now dead. He lives a respectable but dull life in the country, which includes being guardian to his adoptive niece Cecily. In order to get away from this and enjoy himself, he pretends to have a wild brother called Ernest who lives in London, but Jack himself is actually Ernest. His best friend is Algernon and Jack is in love with Algernon's cousin

Gwendolen. Algernon only knows Jack as Ernest and knows nothing about Jack's other life. Algernon himself has an imaginary friend called Bunbury, whom he uses as an excuse when he needs to get out of a tedious social event.

TRIGGER

Algernon has seen Jack's cigarette case with an inscription to 'Uncle Jack' and has begun to suspect that his friend has a double life.

PLOT

Jack tells Algernon he intends to propose to Gwendolen. When challenged about the cigarette case, he tells the whole story of his double life but says he is about to give it up as Cecily is far too interested in Ernest.

First obstacle

Gwendolen accepts Jack's proposal and says that she can only love someone called Ernest, the name she knows him by. Jack immediately resolves to change his name and so appears to have an easy solution to this obstacle.

Second obstacle

Gwendolen's mother, Lady Bracknell, quizzes Jack before she can allow the engagement. He does well until he confesses to being adopted, whereupon she rejects him as a suitor for her daughter. This is a far bigger obstacle for Jack and, although he doesn't seem to have a complete solution, he resolves to announce the death of the fictional Ernest to his family in the country, in preparation for changing his own name to Ernest.

Algernon is determined to meet Cecily and so he turns up at Jack's home pretending to be Ernest.

Subplot

It is obvious that Cecily's governess Miss Prism is in love with the local priest, Dr Chasuble.

Third obstacle

Jack can't tell everyone that Algernon is an impostor because Algernon will reveal Jack's lies. He is obliged to pretend that Algernon is indeed his brother Ernest.

Subplot

Algernon falls in love with Cecily, proposes and is accepted.

Fourth obstacle

Cecily announces that she, too, can only love a man called Ernest. Algernon also decides to have himself christened Ernest.

Fifth obstacle

Gwendolen meets Cecily. Gwendolen and Cecily discover that they are both engaged to Ernest Worthing. This is quickly resolved when Jack and Algernon turn up and it is clear that the women are not both engaged to the same man.

Sixth obstacle

Gwendolen and Cecily both insist on being engaged to Jack's brother Ernest, not Jack and Algernon. This is resolved when Jack admits he has no brother. Both men persist in the idea of changing their name to Ernest, and Gwendolen and Cecily forgive them.

Remaining obstacle

This plot so far has consisted of a series of obstacles that have been fairly easily resolved, apart from the matter of Lady Bracknell refusing to consider Jack as a suitor for Gwendolen. She won't change her mind unless he makes 'a definite effort to produce at any rate one parent, of either sex, before the season is quite over'. Jack seems to have no answer to this, so it is the main obstacle that the plot hinges on.

Final crisis

Lady Bracknell consents to the marriage of her nephew Algernon and Cecily when she hears that Cecily is an heiress. Jack seizes his opportunity and, in his role as Cecily's guardian, refuses his permission for the marriage unless Lady Bracknell also consents to his marriage to Gwendolen. Lady Bracknell refuses and is about to leave. It looks as if all is lost.

This is an important moment. The closer the characters can be taken to the brink of total disaster, the more gripping the plot will be. There is nothing in the play so far to suggest that Jack will find a way to make Lady Bracknell change her mind so he looks to have lost Gwendolen.

Final twist

Cecily's governess Miss Prism is identified as the woman who abandoned Jack as a baby. This means that he can find out something about his parents – in fact, he assumes that Miss Prism is his mother. This shows a more appealing side of Jack's rather flippant nature: he isn't bothered about the possibility of his parents being of a lower class and even accepts that he may be illegitimate.

Resolution

It turns out that Jack is the son of Lady Bracknell's sister and therefore he is Algernon's brother. What's more, his real name is Ernest. He is now able to marry Gwendolen, Algernon can marry Cecily and Miss Prism finally captures Dr Chasuble.

The plot is neatly tied up with everyone paired off and no one punished for their past mistakes. It isn't a particularly funny plot, and the laughs are generated by Oscar Wilde's many witticisms. His characters tend to all speak in the same way, but this hasn't stopped the play from becoming a comedy classic. The string of coincidences, and the idea that two young women would have a rather silly fixation with the name Ernest, can only be made to work in a comedy.

Putting it all together

Once you have a good idea where your plot is going, it's time to start working out the details and putting the events into some sort of sequence.

Focus point

Plot considerations will be different depending on whether you are writing a short story, a sitcom episode or a one-act play. A story can be set anywhere and move around in time and space, a play is constrained by the physical environment of the theatre and a sitcom by the technical considerations of TV. All forms need a degree of discipline to keep the story within the required length.

BACKSTORY

Adam has inherited his Aunt Margaret's share of The House of Relaxation and is moving his own small business into the premises she shared with Laura. Stuart is Laura's receptionist and Wendy is Adam's personal assistant.

TRIGGER

Adam and Wendy are moving in. We learn that Stuart and Wendy are not going to get along. Adam is determined to get his own way with Laura – in particular, he wants the room that she uses, because Margaret's old room is too small for him.

PLOT

Laura leaves for the garden centre, because Margaret said she intended to be reincarnated as a tree. Adam mentions that he has a client due soon, but when Stuart tries to add that to the appointment book Adam shows him their electronic organizer, which speaks the appointments. Stuart is fascinated by the organizer, but has to take a call from a Mr Jamieson asking for an appointment with Laura. Laura returns with a pot plant instead of a tree.

Obstacle one

Laura is determined to hang on to her room, and decides to keep it locked. She also uses the excuse that Stuart would never consent to rearranging the reception area and her room needs to be on the same side as Stuart's desk.

When Stuart is alone, he plays with the organizer and accidentally clears its memory.

Subplot

Mr Jamieson, a brusque businessman, arrives and is incorrectly shown into Laura's office.

Obstacle two

Adam asks Stuart to swap places with Wendy as part of his plan to get Laura's office, but Stuart refuses.

Subplot

Laura and Mr Jamieson talk at cross-purposes. Another client arrives and, as the organizer is blank, Adam assumes it is his client.

Laura's client is beginning to respond to her. Adam's client seems bemused at first but then begins to respond.

Adam instructs Wendy to find a way to swap places with Stuart. Wendy pretends that she can hear Margaret's spirit asking to be on Wendy's side of the room so she moves the pot plant, but then pretends that it's set off her hay fever, meaning that she needs to move away from it. The only option is for her to swap places with Stuart.

Crisis

Both clients are leaving. Laura's client has changed into a New Age type. Adam's client has changed into a businessman but has become so over-confident he doesn't need Adam's help any more. They meet in reception, and it turns out they are father and son who run a family business together.

Ending:

Adam is furious that he's lost the marketing contract. Laura is smug about her success with the businessman. Then they notice that Wendy and Stuart have swapped places. Now Laura is angry and Adam is pleased. Wendy explains that it was all due to Margaret. Laura dumps the pot plant in the waste bin.

Plot detail

Look at all the notes you've made so far and work out the detail of your plot.

Remember

- Characters need to be consistent.
- The plot needs a series of increasingly challenging obstacles.
- It must be difficult for any character to just walk away.
- There must be conflict.
- Keep the exposition to a minimum.
- Don't let the sidekicks and their story take over.
- The ending needs to feel both surprising and inevitable.

Editing

In a real-life situation, you won't work through every single exercise before you start writing. If you're anything like me, you'll be inclined to jump straight in and start writing round a rough idea, realize it isn't working, go back and do some of the prep, then write again, then realize it needs something more, so go back and do some more prep, and so on. This is often quite time wasting, although at other times the writing just flows and the prep isn't needed. You'll work out your own way of doing things but, if it isn't working, you can always go back to the basic exercises and apply them to the piece you're working on.

At some point, do make a step-by-step plan of the plot. Some writers like to do this very early on, while others wait till they've done a rough draft. In either case, once you have your plot dissected and laid out in front of you, it'll be much easier to spot the flaws.

 ## Key idea

For scripts, make a rough model of the set from an old cardboard box, with a slip of paper for each character. Move them round and make sure the plot hangs together.

For most types of storytelling, discipline and economy are what's required, so check that every step of the plot is there for a reason, and that it moves the story forward as well as giving information and revealing character.

Look at each individual scenario and check that it has its own beginning, middle and cliffhanger before the end. Make sure the ending resolves the main plot, ties up the subplots and focuses on the main character or characters.

 ## Key idea

Have a logical reason for everything that happens – but remember that logical is not the same as sensible.

Where to next?

You now have characters and plot for a short piece, but read the next chapter, which runs through the specific requirements of sitcom writing, before you write it out.

11

Sitcoms

For many comedy writers, a successful TV sitcom is their Holy Grail. There are specific requirements for traditional sitcoms, and while some do break new ground, very few move outside the basics of the genre.

In this chapter you will learn how to devise a situation that fulfils the requirements of sitcom, how to create well-rounded, vivid characters, and how to construct plots where the humour comes from the characters' responses to a situation and the tensions in their relationships.

Traditional sitcoms

In a traditional sitcom the core situation, sets and characters don't change, except perhaps very slowly in a long-running sitcom. It generally works best if the situation is a believable one that most viewers can identify with, although of course some sitcoms break the rules. For instance, in *Frasier*, while we might believe that Frasier Crane would give a home to his elderly father, the level of the father's disability in no way justifies the services of a full-time live-in physiotherapist.

Most sitcoms are based around no more than three sets or locations, which are used in every episode. *The Royle Family* never moved outside the family home (except in various specials) and concentrated on the living room, the dining area and the kitchen.

SITUATION

The basic situation for most sitcoms is usually one that will never run out of stories – such as a family or a workplace. However, even the most carefully chosen situation will be limited by time passing: for instance, the young adults who started out flat-sharing in *Friends* were always eventually going to become older people who probably were going to buy houses and have children. Family shows such as *Roseanne*, *Outnumbered* and *My Family* have to adapt to the fact that the actors playing the children will grow up and move away, often leading to convoluted plot twists to keep them in the family home.

Key idea

Just like other types of comedy, sitcoms benefit from a claustrophobic situation.

Is the situation I've already devised for the story of Adam and Laura suitable for a sitcom? If Adam and Laura are both unsuccessful in running their small businesses, it is feasible that they might share premises indefinitely. Wendy works for Adam because she performs so badly in interviews that she can't get another job, and Stuart is too wet to look elsewhere, so he stays with Laura.

Sitcom potential

Look at the situations you've already created and decide whether any of them have good sitcom potential. If not, create one or more new situations.

CHARACTERS

It's been said that sitcoms should be called charactercoms, because it's the characters that matter most.

Sitcom characters never develop and, the longer a series runs, the harder this can be to maintain. It's easier to accept that older characters are set in their ways, which gives sitcoms like *One Foot in the Grave* or *Last of the Summer Wine* a head start. It's harder to believe that the younger characters from *Coupling, Friends* or *Two Pints of Lager and a Packet of Crisps* are still the same several series down the line.

Gavin and Stacey is unusual in that it follows the characters through one of life's journeys (the central characters meet, marry, split up and reunite) but the characters don't change across all three series. This means, of course, that they never learn anything from their experiences – they don't mature or change with the passing of time.

It's also true that sitcom characters, however young, lead routine lives, always going to the same pub and mixing with the same friends. Since this is unrealistic, it can be hard to understand why the format is so enduringly popular – perhaps because we all crave stability and fear change.

Focus point

In a sitcom the aim should be to put strong, well-developed characters into a variety of stories and watch how they cope – always, of course, staying in character.

Jan Etherington, award-winning comedy writer, broadcaster and journalist

'A common mistake new comedy writers make is: to write gags. In situation comedy, the humour should come from the character's response to a situation and the tension of their relationships – not from the 'clunk, clunk – ting!' of your favourite ferret joke.'

Laura is quite a low-profile character because her essentially selfish drive to get her own way is hidden behind her pretend touchy-feelyness. Adam's flaws are more up front, since he is clearly deluded

*about his own success and sex appeal. In the interplay between
these two there is plenty of potential for laughs. Wendy would need
to constantly puncture both Laura's and Adam's pretensions, while
Stuart would be permanently puzzled by the other three characters.*

Key idea

The characters in a sitcom have to be strongly conceived from
the beginning, because there's no room for development.

Sitcom characters

Choose two or three characters for a sitcom. You can use
characters taken from earlier exercises or create new ones. Are
they strong enough to carry a sitcom? Will you be able to create
laughter from their main flaw week after week? (Don't attempt to
write an ensemble piece just yet – stick with just two or three main
characters.)

There are two basic formats for sitcom characters:

1 A single point of focus for every episode – either a single main
   character surrounded by supporting characters, as in *Miranda*, or
   a two-hander such as *Steptoe and Son*
1 An ensemble, such as *'Allo 'Allo!* or *The Thick of It*. All the
   characters have some involvement with every episode, but the
   focus can fall on different characters each week.

RELATIONSHIPS

If the characters in a sitcom are fixed, then so too, are their
relationships. You already know that the characters need to be in
conflict, and they need binding ties. Once you have these two core
factors in place, you can develop the relationships further. When two
characters are together, the dynamics are bound to change if a third
is brought into the scene. Look at all the combinations and decide
how things will pan out between them.

If you find this difficult, try choosing a model on which to base
the relationships. The family is the easiest model to understand,
but you could also use political systems (is this a democracy or a

dictatorship?) or the animal world (is this a herd of wildebeest or a pride of lions?).

Laura, as the oldest, could be a mother figure, albeit a rather selfish one. I see Adam as an annoying brother-in-law, Wendy as a teenager and Stuart as a child. If they were animals in a zoo, Laura would be a member of the cat family, small, sleek and self-centred, Adam an overly energetic monkey, Wendy a not very poisonous snake and Stuart something lovable but slow, like a koala.

How your characters relate to one another

Look at how your characters relate to one another. Decide which model works for their relationship. Can you see the comedy potential?

Miranda Hart, comedy actress and writer

'A common mistake new comedy writers make, in terms of sitcom, is forgetting that story is the most important thing. It might seem fun to write your characters sitting around saying great jokes, but each scene has to go somewhere and move the story on.'

PLOTS AND SUBPLOTS

As you already know, sitcom plots have to be self-contained and circular. A trigger sets each episode in motion, and by the end the issues raised by that trigger must be resolved without changing anything about the central situation.

One advantage of writing for a sitcom is that the story can usually start right on the trigger, because the situation and backstories are given. For example, the *Porridge* episode 'Just Desserts' opens just after the trigger, with Fletcher hunting for his tin of pineapple chunks that has gone missing.

Key idea

The most effective plots are usually the ones that use the characters' central obsessions. For instance, in *Only Fools and Horses* the plots that focused on Del trying to make money, or Rodney trying to improve himself, were more satisfying than plots about their romantic lives. If you keep the plot simple, it will give the characters room to take over.

It isn't essential to include a subplot in a half-hour sitcom. An episode of *Yes Minister* called 'The Greasy Pole' has a plot that runs as straight as an arrow, from the first scene that sets up the need for the Minister to approve a new chemical factory, to the final scene where he finally decides not to approve it. Of course, there are twists along the way, but we only get one story.

Mostly though a subplot helps with both the pacing of the main plot and the suspense, since you can cut to the subplot at crucial moments. In 'Italian for Beginners', an episode of *The IT Crowd*, the main plot is about the mess Jen gets herself into when she pretends to be able to speak fluent Italian, and how Moss helps her. The subplot is about Roy's increasing obsession with his girlfriend's parents, who died in a fire under circumstances that seem to him deeply improbable. The two stories aren't linked and have separate resolutions. You might think that this wouldn't work at all but there are two crucial scenes involving Jen, Moss and Roy in which both the main plot and the subplot are featured, and that is enough to give the episode coherence.

Mindy Glazer, writer and teacher of sitcom writing online

'Sitcoms are not about jokes. They are about character, conflict and action, just like any other good story. Jokes are a way of telling the story. They reveal character, jeopardy and resolution. A sitcom is a story told in jokes the way an opera is a story told in song, but the story comes first.'

The only way to find out whether your sitcom idea has got enough about it to make a series is to rough out at least six plots. I can see plenty of potential episodes for 'The House of Relaxation':

- *Episode 1: Adam and Wendy move into the House of Relaxation offices.*
- *Episode 2: Adam decides the business needs a website, while Laura prefers old-fashioned leaflets. They go head to head over it.*
- *Episode 3: Laura is having money problems, so she decides to write a book about stress management.*
- *Episode 4: Adam's flashy car lets him down. He tries to borrow Laura's Beetle but ends up with Stuart's ancient bicycle.*
- *Episode 5: Laura decides she's a Druid and Christmas is banned, whereas Adam expects to make a whole heap of money with his Christmas marketing ideas.*
- *Episode 6: Laura sets up an alternative dating agency.*
- *And so on.*

Roughing out plots

Work out six rough outlines for plots using your chosen situation and characters.

Putting it all together

Choose a plot

Choose one of your plot outlines (not the opening episode) and work on the trigger and the ending. Remember that the characters have to come full circle, so that nothing changes, while the particular storyline has to be resolved. Decide whether or not your characters will get what they want. Decide whether any of the comedy will be generated by the plot.

Workshop

Put all the elements of a sitcom episode together. Write out the plot in detail and, at each stage, check that:
- each character's behaviour is consistent with their dominant flaw

- the dominant flaw of one or more of the characters is driving the plot
- the characters' relationships with one another are consistent.
- Re-examine the ending and make sure it is in harmony with the style of your sitcom. For instance, if your style is light, don't have a dark ending.
- Finally, check out how you will generate the laughs through the plot, characters and dialogue.

THE OPENING EPISODE

Sitcoms often stand or fall by their first episode. If you, or your actors, have a track record, your audience may be forgiving of a weak opener and may continue to watch, but it's bad policy to rely on that. The opener needs to set everything up and be stonkingly funny. The opening episode of any sitcom is always the hardest one to write because it needs to establish the set-up, and the writer can't assume that the audience already knows what it's all about.

Key idea

Avoid writing the opening episode first. Write one of the other episodes, and then go back to the opener when you've got to know your characters and how they interact.

Think about the opener

Consider how you would write the opening episode of your sitcom. Make a list of everything that could be explained in the opener. Include each character's:

- backstory
- main facets, including their dominant flaw
- situation
- binding ties
- way of interacting with the other characters.

Look through the list and decide what can come out – pare it down to the absolute essentials.

Now decide how the opening episode will set the comedy tone for the rest of the series.

Phil Collinge, comedy writer and radio producer

'It's been said that, "In writing all you need is an original idea – however, it doesn't have to be your own original idea." Well, in comedy it does! Your sitcom idea has to be original, your jokes have to be your own, and you need to develop a style that is all your own (imagine Jimmy Cricket doing Jimmy Carr's routines and you'll see what I mean).'

Start writing

You should now have all the material you need to write a sitcom episode, and from Chapter 10 everything you need to write either a short story or a one-act play. Start writing whichever one of these appeals to you most.

Where to next?

Comedy doesn't have to be frothy and frivolous: sometimes it makes a serious point or deals with painful issues. The next chapter introduces you to the basics of serious comedy writing.

12

Character development and deeper plotting

Comedy can be a serious literary business. In 2010 a comedy won the Mann Booker Prize (*The Finkler Question* by Howard Jacobson). However, a writer can't turn any comedy into a serious work just by adding a message or more developed characters – some comedy is far too frothy and fragile for such treatment. You need to feel the urge to write in this way first, and the comedy will develop from that starting point.

There is nothing to stop you using comedy values to explore deeper issues, either character based or message based (or, of course, both). The work you've produced so far may contain themes – or even obsessions – that are worth exploring in more depth.

In this chapter you will learn how to develop a theme and a message with emotional as well as comic impact, about character development and about how to use humour to make serious points.

Whenever there's a poll trying to find the world's favourite novel invariably James Joyce's *Ulysses* comes out top. And invariably, when pressed, most people who vote for it admit that they haven't read it, or haven't managed to finish it. This is a shame because, while it is a demanding read, it is also a funny book.

Ulysses relies on the comedy technique of bathos (see Chapter 1). Ulysses, or Odysseus as he was originally known, was the legendary ancient Greek hero who fought in the Trojan War, was involved in the Trojan Horse trick and who then took ten adventurous years to travel back to his home in Ithaca. Joyce's novel, on the other hand, is about the far from heroic Leopold Bloom and his journey through one day of his life in Dublin in 1904. Joyce uses the Odysseus journey as a template for Bloom's day. He uses comedy in the plot, the characters and the language:

The sea, the snotgreen sea, the scrotumtightening sea.

 ## Alan Ayckbourn, director and playwright

'Comedy is, in my opinion, writing set out in all seriousness from one individual's viewpoint, which other individuals, to his or her mystification, find funny. You can't actually alter the way you view the world. All you can do is write whatever you want to write truthfully and honestly. It's for others to judge whether your viewpoint is "comic" or "serious". If after a few years no one's laughing, don't despair. You may still be a writer but not necessarily a comic one.'

Any story can be told as either a tragedy or a comedy, and the same themes occur in all forms of storytelling. A man and woman are locked in a bitterly loveless marriage – is this *Who's Afraid of Virginia Woolf* or *Fawlty Towers*? The misery of life in the trenches during the First World War is depicted – *Birdsong* or *Blackadder*?

Theme

If you look at the work you've generated so far you will probably be able to see one or more themes emerging. After all, these are the things you're interested in, so why wouldn't you write about them? Jane Austen was passionately interested in the tension between love and the pressures on women in her time to marry, and so that is what she wrote about. In the twentieth century Kingsley Amis, an equally funny writer, was equally interested in relationships, but he saw everything from a man's point of view.

Sexual politics is a recurring theme of abiding interest to most of us, but you may be far more concerned with global warming or celebrity gossip. There is no point in beating yourself up if your interests seem trivial. If you force yourself to write about deeper issues that don't truly engage you, then your writing will be thin and unconvincing.

Focus point

There is no hiding place for a writer, and once you start to write your personal obsessions will emerge.

Find your themes

Identify any themes that resonate particularly for you.

Message

Whatever your personal themes are, you will also have an attitude to them. If you're interested in global warming, do you think we're headed for Doomsday or do you think it's a fuss about nothing? This is something else you can't fake.

You can choose to write ironically, appearing to support something but all the while quietly undermining it. This was Johnny Speight's intention when he wrote the sitcom *Till Death Us Do Part*. The main character Alf Garnett was held up to ridicule for his outmoded racist and anti-socialist views. Although the series was a huge hit, there was much debate at the time as to whether Speight had succeeded, since viewers who agreed with Alf saw him as an embattled man holding out for what was right.

There's not much we can do about audience reaction to our work. As a writer, you have to focus on what you want to say and hope that the message gets through.

Pinpoint your attitude

Look at each of your themes and decide what your attitude to them is – this will give you your message.

In character-based comedy there is always likely to be a happy ending, because the audience will have engaged with the characters and been amused by them. Message-based comedy can often be much darker. The various conflicts in the 1964 movie *Dr Strangelove or: How I Learned to Stop Worrying and Love the Bomb* are only resolved when the bomb is actually dropped in the last scene, with the implication that the planet is about to be destroyed.

Key idea

If your writing is message driven, you will still need engaging characters to help the audience connect with the story and its message, although you may not need character development.

The blackly comic novel *Slaughterhouse-Five* has a strong anti-war message but the central character is the permanently bewildered and totally non-aggressive Billy Pilgrim. We see the lunacy of war through his eyes. *Catch 22* uses a more straightforward comedic technique to pursue the same theme, with a central character who doesn't accept the status quo. The protagonist Yossarian takes the war personally, and constantly asks why people are trying to kill him. Both Billy Pilgrim and Yossarian are versions of the innocent comedy character who sees the world differently from the rest of us.

In *Hard Times,* Dickens uses comedy techniques to make his critique of industrial society palatable to an audience that would have been largely either unaware of or indifferent to the sufferings of the industrial poor. However, the main characters are not comedy characters at all and there is little character development. Gradgrind and his daughter Louisa do change in the course of the novel, but most of this happens off stage.

Where is your passion?

Look through the work you've written so far to see whether any of the material connects with the topics you feel passionately about. The chances are that these issues have already come through in the work you did just to generate laughs.

Characters

Serious literary writers usually aim for character development in their main characters. The protagonist is on a journey, and at the end of the story they will have changed in some significant way. Characters such as Raskolnikov and Madame Flaubert are taken through an extreme series of events that have profound effects on them. However, not all novels and dramas work this way: some protagonists such as Sherlock Holmes and Hercule Poirot don't develop, and their appeal lies in their consistency.

Key idea

In comedy, the balance is very much in favour of characters like Bertie Wooster that don't develop and – as we've already seen – in sitcom, character development is positively forbidden.

Indeed, character development can create problems for a writer. When Nigel Williams wrote *The Wimbledon Poisoner*, he tracked his central character, Henry Farr, through something of a midlife crisis and out the other side to a peaceful resolution. However, later on, when he had the idea for *Scenes from a Poisoner's Life*, he had to undo much of his good work and make Henry unhappy again.

Nevertheless, there is character development in some comedy. In *Pride and Prejudice*, both of the central characters go through a process of learning about their own tendencies to pride and prejudice, and come out of it as more mature people who are ready for married life. In *The Importance of Being Earnest*, Jack Worthing has to let go of his hypocritical double life in order to find happiness. In *Men in Black*, Will Smith's character Agent J develops from a raw recruit to a fully trained agent. These examples may cover the full spectrum from serious literature to light entertainment but they still have certain basic values in common.

Look at your characters

Look back at the work you've already generated and identify which characters have the potential for development.

Conflict

Conflict remains crucially important. In *Pride and Prejudice* we meet Elizabeth Bennet just at the moment when she is forced to confront a major conflict. She is of the right age to marry, and she soon finds a conflict between her desire to marry for love and the expectations of society and some of her family that she will marry for money and security. She receives a marriage proposal from Mr Collins, whom she doesn't love or even like. She refuses him, despite the fact that marrying him would create a secure future for her entire family. This establishes her as a strong-willed and possibly even selfish person who brushes aside conflict with society. Her dealings with other people are rarely conflicted either, since she is naturally assertive and confident.

It is only when she starts to be drawn to Mr Darcy that she suffers internal conflict. She hates him, she turns down his first proposal, she learns the truth about some of his actions, and eventually she faces her own prejudices against him. Her internal conflict and the plot combine together to take her on this journey.

A journey of some sort is the key to a character-based story. In Elizabeth's case it is a journey to enlightenment and a happy ending. The comedy in *Pride and Prejudice* doesn't come from her journey, however, but from other aspects of the story. The large cast of secondary characters are all funny in different ways. Elizabeth herself is witty, in the sparkling style later associated with Oscar Wilde:

> To find a man agreeable whom one is determined to hate! –
> Do not wish me such an evil.

And it's easy to forget, in the light of so many sexually charged adaptations of the book, that Mr Darcy is a ridiculous character in the opening chapters, and there to be laughed at.

Get serious for a moment

Look back to Chapter 3 and the list of things that make you angry. Choose a topic from the list and write a short serious piece examining why this is. Write about the topic itself and also explain why it means so much to you.

Using comedy for serious issues

Explore in general terms how you might use comedy to write about your topic.

- Start by listing any inherent absurdities and incongruities. This will show you where there is potential for irony.
- Next, consider what sort of characters you could use and what situation you would put them in.
- Think about conflict, for both the characters and the plot.
- How would you make the topic accessible to an audience? Is it something that you suspect most people are in sympathy with, or would you need to find a way to win them over?
- How far could you push things; how far could you let your anger show?

Emotional impact

When you put theme and message together, you arrive at the emotional impact of a piece of writing. In *Hard Times*, Dickens's themes were his usual one of childhood plus a less usual theme of the Industrial Revolution. His messages, briefly put, were that young children can be ruined by their early education and that industrial society is an unnatural and soul-destroying way to live. The emotional impact of these messages is clearly negative, and as a result Dickens struggles to achieve his usual happy ending. Character-based comedy will still have an underlying message – *Pride and Prejudice* explores the theme of the marriage market and the message arising from the happy ending is that it is worth holding out for what you want in life.

Key idea

Theme plus message equals emotional impact.

Plotting

In *Pride and Prejudice*, both Elizabeth and Darcy are on a journey that takes them from mutual dislike, through a learning process about their own failings, to the destination of love and marriage. That journey isn't possible without the events of the story, and in that sense the plot consists of two elements: the sequence of events and the journey of the characters. The same is true if your piece is message driven. You'll need a plot that carries the audience through the piece and one that also displays your message.

Key idea

The simple business of what happens next is what holds the attention of the audience, but it is the deeper story, the journey of the characters, that creates satisfaction.

Simon Brett, writer

'A lot of people get comedy wrong. They think: "Wouldn't it be funny if A B C D happened?" A much better starting point is: "Wouldn't it be tragic if it weren't funny if A B C D happened?"'

In *Hard Times*, Dickens runs several plots in parallel with inevitable complexity. There are two main plots. One tracks the story of the affluent Gradgrind family and the complete failure of Mr Gradgrind's fact-driven system of education, which turns his son into a criminal and leads his daughter into a bitterly unhappy marriage. The other plot follows the desperately hard life of worker Stephen Blackpool and his tragic death.

There is not much comedy there, and yet Dickens uses comedy techniques throughout. For instance, this is how he sucks the reader into his story. On the first page there is an amusing description of Mr Gradgrind:

> …square wall of a forehead, which had his eyebrows for its base, while his eyes found commodious cellarage in two dark caves, overshadowed by the wall… hair, which bristled on the skirts of his bald head, a plantation of firs to keep the wind from its shining surface, all covered with knobs, like the crust of a plum pie…

Having introduced Gradgrind, Dickens now wants to show us the miserable place that is his school, where small children become 'little pitchers' to be filled up with facts. But he doesn't want to frighten his readers off at this early stage, so he continues in a humorous vein:

'Girl number twenty unable to define a horse!' said Mr Gradgrind, for the general behoof of all the little pitchers. 'Girl number twenty possessed of no facts, in reference to one of the commonest of animals!...'

As the story unfolds, comedy takes a back seat, although Dickens is always ready to bring it forward in describing people, and also when he is at his angriest. Here he is describing the reluctance of mill owners to treat their workers decently:

Surely there never was such fragile china-ware as that of which the millers of Coketown were made. Handle them never so lightly, and they fell to pieces with such ease that you might suspect them of having been flawed before. They were ruined when they were required to send labouring children to school; they were ruined when inspectors were appointed to look into their works; they were ruined when such inspectors considered it doubtful whether they were quite justified in chopping people up with their machinery; they were utterly undone when it was hinted that perhaps they need not always make quite so much smoke.

Note that in the last sentence there is a list of four things, and the third item is the most powerful – Dickens is using the most basic of comedy techniques.

Focus point

Be absolutely sure who your protagonists are and make sure they are the focus of the main plot, and particularly the ending.

Subplots

Subplots need just as much thought and input as a main plot. The longer and more complex a work, the more important subplots become, although they must never overwhelm the main story. You can use subplots to maintain a comedy tone – as the main stories in *Hard Times* grow darker, Dickens keeps Mrs Sparsit's subplot firmly comedic:

...whether she would be plaintive or abusive, tearful or tearing; whether she would break her heart, or break the looking-glass; Mr Bounderby could not at all foresee.

You can use subplots to expand on the underlying theme of your piece. The main plot has the function of carrying the story forward, so it is often action driven, whereas in a subplot there is more room for manoeuvre. Joseph Heller uses multiple subplots in *Catch 22* and each one contributes something to the main theme. The death of Snowden is the catalyst for change in Yossarian; the way Orr escapes the war shows that Catch 22 can be beaten, and so on.

Examine your plot ideas

Turn your attention to the plot.

- Can any of your existing plot ideas carry the weight of a substantial story?
- How would you need to expand your plot to make a full-length piece?
- Alternatively, do you need to create a new plot?
- Can you devise one or more subplots that also explore your chosen topic?
- Can you see comedy potential in your plotting?

Imagery

You've already learned quite a lot about imagery, which is simply a way of using language to describe one thing in terms of another. Comedy writers play with imagery all the time. Possibly the most well-known image in English is 'I wandered lonely as a cloud'. If you wrote 'I wandered lonely as the geeky kid with glasses on Sports Day' you'd get two comedy hits, one from playing with a well-known image and one from the new image you've created.

Of course, you have the option of creating your own new images. In *Hard Times*, Dickens summarized the deeply unnatural nature of industrial life in one memorable image that manages to be both funny and sad at the same time:

> The piston of the steam-engine worked monotonously up and down, like the head of an elephant in a state of melancholy madness.

Images become even more effective if they are structured and organized. Dickens adds another animal image by describing coils of smoke as serpents. And as Stephen Blackpool's story approaches its dreadful crisis, he brings the images together:

> The smoke-serpents were indifferent who was lost or found, who turned out bad or good; the melancholy mad elephants... abated nothing of their set routine, whatever happened.

150

IMAGERY AND ALLEGORY

You can treat your entire plot as an image. This is particularly useful if you are trying to convey a message, but it needs to be subtly done. Allegory, as this type of writing is known, is not as popular as it once was. Audiences now resist being lectured at, although the comedy element may help you slip the message past them.

This was Swift's intention when he wrote *Gulliver's Travels*. Gulliver's journey from one bizarre culture to the next is a progress through the various wickednesses of mankind, and when he finally finds a truly civilized society it is run by horses, with human beings reduced to foul and uncontrollable apes. There is much that's amusing in the story, but the message is as dark as it gets.

IMAGERY AND SYMBOLISM

Every time you use an image, you're assuming that the audience will bring something to it. Dickens's melancholy mad elephant depends very much on the fondness English readers feel for elephants. After all, we've only seen them in zoos, and have never had our crops trampled or been terrified by a bull elephant on the rampage. A melancholy mad fox would not produce the same effect at all for us.

Symbolism takes this concept even further. The writer deliberately chooses images that they know will have resonance for the audience. For instance, *Dr Strangelove* is packed with sexual imagery, from the shots of a plane refuelling in mid-air to the phallic cigars given to the most aggressive characters. The idea behind this is that the same urges that fuel a man's sex drive also fuel the aggression that leads to war.

Lesley Bown, writer

'*Sometimes when I'm writing, I keep being distracted by irrelevant jokes and ideas. The only cure, for me, is to write them down. Once, I had so many extras that I wrote a whole new play with them.*'

Workshop

You now have a broad outline for a substantial piece that explores an issue you feel strongly about.

- Examine the emotional impact of your theme and message.
- Rough out the plot and subplots.
- Decide whether using imagery and symbolism would benefit your piece.
- Look in detail at character development for your protagonist.
- Decide how the piece will end, and how the ending will reinforce the message.

Where to next?

Detailed editing is one of the things that separates the amateur writer from the professional, so that's where we're going next.

13

Editing, polishing and unblocking

Any writer who is satisfied with their first draft is either a fool or a genius. The rest of us have to find the energy for editing, rewriting and polishing. This is true of all forms of writing but comedy writers have an extra problem – once you've read through a piece several times you can lose all sense of how funny it is.

The first thing to do, if the deadline allows, is take a break. Work on something else, do some research or networking for a while, then come back to the piece refreshed. Before you start editing, save the original under a different name. That way you can always come back to it, and knowing that will encourage you to be ruthless.

In this chapter you'll learn how to edit and polish your draft, how to keep going and how to deal with problems such as writer's block.

Focus point

Use the exercises in this chapter after you have finished the first draft of your short piece.

We've already looked at editing jokes and editing a sketch, and the same principles apply to editing a longer piece. And here's where the fun really starts, because you'll find that every change you make has a knock-on effect throughout the piece. You'll need to check, check and check again that everything still hangs together after you've finished editing.

Key idea

If you start to lose the sense of your work as funny, all you can do is keep faith with your original vision and carry on with the editing process.

Sue Limb, comedy writer (Dulcie Domum, *Up the Garden Path*, *The Wordsmiths at Gorsemere*)

'The most common mistake new comedy writers make is being prickly and possessive about a piece of work and hyper-sensitive to criticism. Sometimes you just have to throw stuff out and start again.'

Stages of editing

Edit your piece in a systematic way, in stages.

1 READ THROUGH

Read your piece right through once before you do any editing, to give yourself an overview.

2 WRITE TIGHT

Next, remove anything irrelevant, and rewrite anything that's too wordy. Pay special attention to your favourite bits. They may or may not be brilliant, but because you like them you'll be reluctant to make changes, so try to look at them objectively.

If you're writing for performance, reduce the directions to the minimum, only keeping those that are crucial. Most of us include far too many directions because as we write we visualize the performance. With prose, only tell your reader what they need to know, as opposed to what you needed to know as the writer. For both prose and performance, check that the exposition is both crisp and subtle.

Key idea

Be prepared to 'murder your darlings'.

Start with the obvious

Now that you have an overview of your piece, spend some time correcting any obvious problems.

1. Look through your notes and deal with the issues raised.
2. Delete anything irrelevant or unnecessary, including stage directions.
3. Rewrite anything that's too long and wordy (but remember that sometimes wordiness creates laughs).
4. If there's anything you especially love, make sure it needs to be there and is as tightly written as possible.
5. Check the early exposition – ask yourself whether anything can be left till later in the piece.

3 LOOK DEEP

Once you've done the initial tidy up, you can see the piece much more clearly. Think about your original intentions. You may have done what you set out to do, or you may have ended up with something entirely different, but in either case the writing needs to be consistent. So look at the theme, the message and the emotional impact. Check that they hang together and that the ending is appropriate.

 Key idea

Even a lightweight piece will have an element of deeper structure, so it's worth doing this check.

 Run checks

- Look at the theme, the message and the emotional impact of the piece.
- Check that the ending is appropriate and conveys the message.

4 PLAY DEVIL'S ADVOCATE

Ask as many awkward questions as you can about the plot. Why did it happen this way? Why not another way? Why did he say that, why didn't she do this, what were they thinking of when they did the other? If the answer is just 'because it's funnier that way', then think again, because it'll be even funnier if you can make everything appear to be entirely logical.

 Examine your plot

Take a step back from your plot and examine it objectively.

- Write out your plot as a timeline, showing each step along the way for both the what-happens-next part of the plot and the deeper journey that runs in parallel.
- Ask awkward questions about the plot.
- Examine the plot for loopholes.
- Check that the plot is physically possible (e.g. allow time for characters to make journeys).

5 BE CONSISTENT

Check that the characters are consistent on every level – in appearance, vocabulary, attitudes and behaviour. Sometimes you may choose to make a character inconsistent, but never let it happen accidentally or because it suits the plot. External characteristics are easy enough to check, but behaviour is harder. If a character changes their behaviour it needs to be as a result of events in the plot, such as when hard-nosed businessman Mr Jamieson turns into a pussycat due to Laura's soothing therapy (see Chapter 10 and Appendix F).

Check the characters

Look at each character separately and check that they are consistent in their:

- external characteristics
- conflict
- motivation and dominant desire
- flaws.

If there are inconsistencies, either correct them or make sure that there is a good reason for them. Decide whether the audience needs to know about the reason or whether it's enough for you to know.

6 LOOK AT LANGUAGE

Each character should have a way of phrasing things and a typical vocabulary. If you're writing prose, you also need to check the authorial voice, or the character voice if it's in the first person.

Check the language

- Check the language for each character: it needs to be consistent unless there is a reason for it to change.
- For prose, check the consistency of the authorial voice.

7 MARK THE LAUGHS

Whatever you're writing, you need to know where the laughs are. Some types of comedy are more likely to raise a smile than a belly laugh, but you still need to have an understanding of the rhythms of the humour.

Kev F. Sutherland, comedian and comic artist

'If I had to give just one piece of comedy writing advice it would be: find out if your work is funny. For a stand-up this is easy, you do it in front of people and if they laugh, you're funny. That was where the Sitcom Trials came from, subjecting sitcom writing to the same test a stand-up has to go through, letting the audience tell you what works and what doesn't. For my comic strip work it is harder, and it's quite possible I've never had feedback telling me how funny my comic strips are. Gulp. Maybe they're not?'

How easy was that then?

I suspect I've made the whole writing process sound pretty easy. A few lists, a bit of lateral thinking, some writing and editing and, hey presto, you're a comedy writer. But if it was that easy, wouldn't everyone be doing it?

Focus point

At every stage you can find yourself struggling for one reason or another and there will always be times when only willpower, or obsession, keep you going.

TIME

Creative writing takes a particular kind of stamina. As with any
other project, you start in a rush of enthusiasm but can simply run
out of steam after a while. It's important to keep going at these
times, even if progress is slow.

Focus point

It can help to have a writing routine, with specific times set
aside for getting down to it.

Some writers like to create a timetable, so they know when they're
due to finish the first draft, or they have a deadline for a certain
number of words. Breaking the task down into small achievable
units can help, so that you have a sense of progress as each one is
ticked off.

It takes most writers between two weeks and a month to write a
half-hour sitcom episode. Many novelists think in terms of two years
for a novel. If you're realistic about the timescale, you're less likely
to become disheartened and give up.

Key idea

One way of increasing your productivity is this: never end a writing session on a full stop. Always leave something that will help you get started quickly next time – the first sentence of the next bit, or some notes about it.

Finding time

Now you've tried writing comedy, you'll have an idea of how easy or hard it is to find the time.

- Did you struggle to make the time for writing?
- Would it help to get up half an hour earlier in the morning?
- Or go to bed half an hour later?
- Do you remember to use your notebook?
- Do you prefer thinking about writing to actually writing?

BLOCKAGE

Is writer's block a myth? Surely, if you want to write, you'll just do it, won't you? Well, maybe, just like people who want to get fitter join a gym, and then never go there. We all fantasize about the wonderful things we're going to do in the future, and then give up when we find out how difficult it gets. That's one explanation for writer's block, and only you can decide whether to tough it out or give up.

Another explanation may be that, for whatever reason, you just don't want to write the next bit. If that's the case, make brief notes for it and move on to something else. There's no rule that says the writing process has to be linear. This kind of block is often caused by your mind focusing on another part of the work that you really want to write. Once you've got that out of the way, there's a good chance the block will be gone.

Sometimes you can feel blocked because you're trying to think about too many things at once. Take a moment to clear your mind of anything that isn't relevant to the next few sentences, whether they're connected with your writing project or with your life outside writing.

Writing is a solitary business and sometimes it helps to share things with other writers. Having contact with people who understand your difficulties and frustrations is always helpful, and if you're lucky you'll find that their enthusiasm and excitement are contagious. Phone, email or meet up with your writing friends as a way of kick-starting your writing.

Where to next?

The next chapter takes you through the differences between various media.

14

Writing for different media

You probably already know what sort of comedy you want to write, and for which medium. Perhaps you can already see yourself collecting your Bafta, the Man Booker Prize or an Oscar. But have you given any thought to the specific requirements of each type of comedy writing? There is a certain amount of crossover, and the more successful you are the more likely it is that your sitcom will move from TV to radio (or vice versa), that your novel will be filmed, or that your journalism will be published in book form.

In this chapter you will learn about writing for a range of different media, including live and recorded performance, print media and the Internet.

Focus point

This chapter gives some brief guidelines about various media and refers you to other books in this series that go into greater detail.

At the beginning of your career, you'll almost certainly have a lot more rejection than success but, once you've sent a piece to every possible outlet, you can consider rewriting it or rejigging the original idea for a different medium. This gives you a whole new set of opportunities. However, don't rush into this – get to know your chosen medium in depth first, and then branch out.

From a writer's perspective, many of the differences between media are technical, but we should also bear in mind the idea that 'the medium is the message'. This concept was first floated in the 1960s by Marshall McLuhan and, sidestepping the ongoing philosophical debate about it, we can take it to mean that the medium influences how the message is perceived. How often have you been disappointed by the movie of your favourite book? Or bought a book based on a TV series and been equally disappointed?

Key idea

In the transistion from one medium to another, something is always lost. Other things may be gained, but the end result is different and will be experienced differently by the audience.

Every now and then, though, it does work, and that's because the writer and anyone else involved were sensitive to the differences between the two media concerned (the stage musical *Mamma Mia!* and the movie version are an excellent example of a successful transition). All of this is as true for comedy as for any other type of writing.

Different media

Make a list of items that you've experienced in more than one medium – maybe you read the book and saw the film, or went to the musical and saw the film, or watched the TV programme then read the book.

- Which version of each one did you prefer?
- Why?
- Which version had the most popular success? Why do you think that is?

Ken Rock, President, British Society of Comedy Writers

'A common mistake new comedy writers make is thinking their work cannot be altered to suit other formats. It can. Also, don't think there are only one or two markets to send your work to. There are many markets that accept new writers. You have to find them. They won't come to you.'

From novel to TV to radio

Some years ago I wrote a stage play with Ann Gawthorpe that was packed with characters and incident. We decided that it had the makings of a novel and so we created a new, longer plot. Here's an extract:

As soon as Hermione stomped out of the hall and Joyce left to find her tourists something strange happened to the suit of armour. It appeared to come to life. It creaked, moved, and swore.

'Damn,' it said, 'dropped it.' There was a certain amount of scuffling about and then the musical tones of a mobile phone being dialled.

'Hello? Betting World? This is Savile Kingsford.'

The suit of armour was a fake. Far from being medieval, it was designed in the 1950s as a cocktail cabinet. The late-lamented butler had removed the shelves, the bottle holders and the music box that played Greensleeves, added a strategic dent and successfully passed the thing off as medieval. As the whole of the back was hinged it had become Savile's favourite hiding place. Unfortunately, Joyce, in her distraction, was taking the tour backwards and Savile was no longer alone.

'... and if you would like to follow me now,' she was saying, 'we will go into the main hall, and here, as you can see, we have all the family portraits, starting with Sir Richard Kingsford, 1358 to 1418 who built the manor, right up to the present-day owner Lady Hermione, pictured here in her debutante's ballgown.' The tourists followed her, unimpressed.

'The other main feature of the hall is the family collection of armour,' she went on. 'Over here, we have the suit worn by Sir Brawdly Kingsford at the battle of Agincourt. And here you can see the dent where the fatal arrow struck him in the codpiece.'

'No, don't put me on hold,' said the suit of armour, 'I need to talk to Stibbs…'

Joyce nearly jumped out of her skin. Fortunately, the tourists were all Japanese and they assumed that talking armour was just some electronic gadget.

'Oh, Mr Savile,' Joyce said, 'I didn't see you there.' There was a loud clang as Savile banged his head and a smaller one as he dropped his phone again.

'Oh, Joyce, is that you? I was, um, just checking it for rust.'

We then realized that the new plot would also work on TV, although it meant losing a lot of the detail we'd enjoyed putting into the novel. In this extract, the audience already knows that Savile needs a quiet place to make his surreptitious phone call to the bookmaker:

Scene 4. Interior. Stone-flagged hall. Day.

[Three walls are covered in portraits, the other has pikes, swords and shields on it. Around the room are full-sized suits of armour. Joyce is standing surrounded by tourists. She is indicating one of the portraits.]

JOYCE: …and here as you can see, we have all the family portraits, starting with Sir Richard Kingsford, 1358 to 1418, who built the manor, right up to the present-day owner Lady Hermione, pictured here in her debutante's ballgown.

[The camera zooms in on one of the suits of armour. We hear a mobile phone being dialled.]

SAVILE: (*whispering*) Hello? This is Savile Kingsford.

[Joyce, followed by the tourists, moves across to the suit of armour]

JOYCE: The other main feature of the hall is the family collection of armour. Over here we have the suit worn by Sir Brawdly Kingsford at the Battle of Agincourt. And here you can see the dent where the fatal arrow struck him in the codpiece.

SAVILE: (*whispering*) No, don't put me on hold.

[Joyce and the tourists react in amazement]

SAVILE: (*whispering louder*) I said don't put me on hold.

TOURIST #1: Is it haunted?

[Joyce taps loudly on the armour. We hear the sound of a mobile phone being dropped inside a suit of armour.]

SAVILE: Ouch! What, who's there?

[Savile lifts up the visor and peers out]

JOYCE: Mr Savile!

SAVILE: I was, um, just checking it for rust, Joyce.

It didn't seem too much of a jump to turn the TV script into a radio script, although this particular scene gave us a few problems. Even though the phone call to the bookie has been set up, will the listeners actually twig that Savile is inside the suit of armour?

Scene 4. Int. Morning

Atmos: Stone-flagged hall

F/X: People murmuring (under), footsteps

JOYCE: And if you would like to follow me now, we will go into the main hall, and here, as you can see, we have all the family portraits, starting with Sir Richard Kingsford, 1358 to 1418, who built the manor, right up to the present-day owner Lady Hermione, pictured here in her debutante's ballgown.

F/X: People murmuring (under), mobile phone dialling inside a suit of armour

SAV: (*whispering*) Hello? Betting World? This is Savile Kingsford.

JOYCE: The other main feature of the hall is the family collection of armour. Over here we have the suit worn by Sir Brawdly Kingsford at the Battle of Agincourt. And here you can see the dent where the fatal arrow struck him in the codpiece.

SAV: (*whispering*) No, don't put me on hold again. Just tell me whether Burdock collected my winnings, sorry, his winnings.

F/X: Piece of armour dropping on flagstone

JOYCE: Oh, Mr Savile, I didn't see you in there.

SAV: (*whispering*) So who was it that picked them up?

JOYCE: Er... would you like us to come back when you've finished your phone call?

F/X: Mobile phone being dropped inside suit of armour

SAV: Ouch! What, who's there?

F/X: Clanking armour

JOYCE: Shall I hold the helmet while you get out?

F/X: Clanking armour

SAV: I was, um, just checking it for rust, Joyce.

You can see that the same story is told in different ways depending on the medium.

Writing for performance

Writing for performance is about more than just the words. The performers will add to the comedy at many levels: just the way someone looks, their hair and clothes, will have an effect on the audience. The performer's body language creates another level, and physical comedy is an art form in its own right. Inevitably this means that the performance will be different from the pictures you saw in your head as you were writing. It also means that the more you understand about performance the more accurate those pictures are likely to be.

Key idea

Performers add timing, rhythm and, in live media, sensitivity to the audience to your script.

Focus point

The best way to gain an understanding of performance is to try it yourself, for instance at a local open-mic night or in an amateur dramatic group. Or follow the example of young comedian Bo Burnham and post a video of yourself online.

Apart from radio (see below), performance is intensely visual and scripts need to reflect that. Characters reveal themselves through their actions as much as their words.

Changing media

In Chapter 4 you looked at an extract from *The Diary of a Nobody*. Work out how you could rewrite it as a dialogue for the stage.

- Would you keep all the characters?
- What actions and body language would you include?
- How would you treat the first paragraph?

Count Arthur Strong, via Steve Delaney

'Although everything should, of course, be a collaboration, amazingly the writer's contribution is often overlooked or undervalued. Never forget, without them there are no words to say. Try that hat on for size, all you actors and directors!'

Recorded performance

Apart from radio, costs are high in recorded media. Bear this in mind when you're deciding about outside filming, special effects and so on. More than anywhere else, the writer is part of a team and the director (or, in radio, the producer) will have as much or even more creative input. The piece is created at the editing stage rather than at the writing stage.

It's important to gain an understanding of the role of the camera in TV and movies. It moves, taking the viewer with it. It creates point of view (usually abbreviated to 'pov') so that the viewer can see events from the perspective of more than one character. It also allows for close-ups, taking the viewer right into the characters' emotions and responses.

TELEVISION

Television comedy is the most easily accessible for most of us, and so it tends to set the benchmark. It's so easy to change channels that it's important to grab the attention of the audience immediately, and keep their interest going. Sometimes there is a studio audience to give a live feel that helps the actors, but where there is no studio audience the performers may need a fuller script to help them find their rhythm. TV performances are small and intimate. (For more on this, see *Masterclass: Writing a TV Sitcom, Getting It Produced* and *Masterclass: Writing Plays,* which has a chapter on TV.)

Key idea

Rehearsal time is short for TV, so performers need to get into the script and find the laughs immediately.

Revisit your sketch

In Chapter 8 you wrote a short sketch. The medium wasn't specified, but no doubt you had either TV or stage in mind as you wrote. Check that the sketch does work for your chosen medium, and then rewrite it for the other one.

MOVIES

In the UK, movies have low budgets compared with the US, sine the market is so much smaller, and so comedy has to come from the interactions between characters rather than from expensive location filming or special effects. *Shaun of the Dead* is a good example.

Since the audience can't change channels and they've paid for their seats, they will usually be willing to give the movie a chance. Once a movie goes to DVD, of course, it will be watched at home like TV.

Focus point

Movie audiences are less likely to be distracted than those watching TV at home, and in fact they will need time to settle into their seats and get focused – this is the job of the opening credits and the first few moments of the action.

Plots usually have to be constructed in great detail using a technique known as storyboarding. This is rather like drawing out the plot in cartoon form. The director has pretty well total control of a movie, and both in the shooting and the editing processes the original script can be changed beyond recognition. (For more on this, see *Get Started in Screenwriting* and *Complete Screenwriting Course.*

RADIO

Radio is a unique medium and in the UK the BBC has a long history of delivering all kinds of comedy on radio. Radio audiences are loyal but are often listening at home while getting on with other tasks, or in the car. Catch their interest from the opening moments or they'll be likely to change stations or turn the radio off.

Radio scriptwriters have virtually limitless freedom in their choice of locations, sound effects and music. You can have as many sets as you want, furnished with no regard to budget. You can be in the Cleopatra's palace one moment and on the moon the next. On the other hand, there is the discipline of conveying everything with sound, predominantly dialogue.

> ## Key idea
>
>
> In radio, dialogue has to reveal character, move the plot forward, convey information and, of course, create laughs.

Don't bring on characters in groups; allow time for the listener to get used to each new voice. Find ways to repeat the characters' names from time to time.

Sound effects and background sounds help with these tasks. We learn something if a character shuts a door with a quiet click, or slams it. The plot is moved forward if the sound of a car's engine is interrupted by the sound of the car crashing. Information comes from background noises such as an owl hooting or waves crashing on a seashore. All of these can also create laughs if used in the right way.

We can also, of course, hear the character's thoughts, as long as the listener is always quite clear that it's the inner voice they're hearing. Music can also be used to create laughs, usually by being quite inappropriate for the scene. (For more on this, see *Masterclass: Writing Plays*, which has a chapter on writing for radio.)

> ## Check out your plot
>
>
> In Chapter 10 you created the plot for either a one-act play or a short story.
> - Are you sure the plot works for your chosen medium?
> - How would you adapt it for the other one?

Live performance

Live performance has to be bigger and broader than performance for a camera. Don't make the mistake of assuming that an audience can see small movements and subtle facial expressions – although the use of repeater screens (large screens in the auditorium that show the performance as it happens) is changing the nature of live performance, especially stand-up. With or without screens, the interaction between performers and audience means that no two nights will ever be the same, and your script will have good days and bad days.

THEATRE

Like a cinema audience, theatre audiences need a little time to settle down but are then likely to give the play, sketch show or stand-up their full attention.

There is a longer rehearsal period for theatre than for movies or TV, and also plays are often given an out-of-town try-out with the specific aim of fine-tuning the script. This doesn't mean that you can send in a rough draft. Always send your best work, but accept the opportunity to polish it even further. (For more on this, see *Masterclass: Writing Plays*.)

Write an opening

In Chapter 12 you created the outline for a substantial piece. Now write the opening:

- as a novel
- as a play.

COMEDY CLUBS

Comedy clubs are where most stand-up comics start their careers and it's quite a different environment and different audience from a theatre or concert hall. The entertainment is a just a part of the whole experience, which includes drinks and socializing. This means that the audience is likely to be more restless, with people constantly going to the bar or the toilets, and less focused, since they are likely to be interacting with the people around them.

Alcohol loosens the tongue, as we all know, so heckling is likely to be more frequent and possibly more aggressive. As the writer, you can only do a certain amount to protect the performer from all this, but a strong, funny script and a few heckle responses worked out in advance will give them a good start. (For more on this, see *Get Started in Stand-Up*.)

Print

In contrast to performance, experiencing print media is usually a solitary experience. Words and images on a page or screen give the writer a direct line to the reader's mind. A reader can look back and read again if they get confused about a plot or just don't get a joke. Equally, they can dip in and out as they feel like it.

JOURNALISM

Humorous journalism is usually in the form of a regular weekly or monthly column. Pieces are short, between 500 and 1,000 words. Rather like a sketch, a short, humorous piece will usually have a single connecting thread that leads the reader to a surprise ending. An eye-catching title is the best way to persuade readers to stop at the column and read it. (For more on this, see *Get Your Articles Published*.)

Revisit your stand-up routines

In Chapter 6 you created stand-up routines. Rewrite one of them as a humorous magazine piece.

NOVELS

Someone picking up a novel has chosen to spend some time reading and brings a certain amount of willingness to engage with the story – although they will soon put the book down if they aren't enjoying it. The plot can develop as quickly or as slowly as you choose, but there must be something on every page to keep the reader interested. (For more on this, see *Get Started in Writing a Novel*.)

Ken Rock, President, British Society of Comedy Writers

'*Don't give up. If your script is rejected it doesn't mean it's no good. It's just not right for that person.*'

THE INTERNET

Initially, Internet reading seemed to be about finding a website by chance, looking quickly round and then moving on, but gradually readers have started to develop loyalties and will return to their favourites.

Understanding how to write for the Internet in still in its infancy. It's become clear that readers prefer to click rather than scroll, so think in terms of enough words to fill one screen. Internet readers have very short attention spans so you need to get their attention immediately. Short paragraphs and short sentences are much easier to cope with when we read on screen.

A blog is a good way to get your humour out there. Don't waffle, or use the blog for different purposes – if you build up a following for your wacky comedy, don't suddenly start blogging about the cute things your toddler said or the irritation you feel about traffic jams. (For more on this, see *Get Started in Self-publishing*.)

 Get blogging

Start a blog, using your own life as the basis for humour.

Where to next?

You probably aren't interested in writing just for the fun of it – you want to see your work out there, and you want to make people laugh. The next chapter looks at how to go about placing your work.

15

The practicalities of placing your work

People write for all sorts of reasons – fame, fortune, therapy, compulsion. Some people know from the very beginning that they are aiming for an audience; others don't realize until later that they need to get their work out there. I suspect that very few writers are completely satisfied with the process of writing and are content even if no one else ever sees their work. Of course, there's no real way of knowing, since by definition they are unknown to the wider world. However, on the assumption that you would like to reach an audience, this chapter offers a few tips on how to go about it.

You will learn about the unpaid ways of getting your work in front of an audience, about the submissions process and how to advance your career.

Tony Staveacre, writer/producer in TV, radio and theatre

'The most common mistake new comedy writers make is to try to get inside the mind of the commissioning editor on whose opinion the future of a project will depend. This is impossible. Anyway, you really don't want to go there. Look at the sequence of rejection slips that all great classic comedy ideas have collected before they hit the mark. P. G. Wodehouse papered the walls of his bedroom with rejection slips. Accept the grim fact that most commissioning editors are idiots who have no sense of humour. Make it your plan to find the one salaried suit who is on your wavelength. That will take a bit of determined research.'

Working for free

There are many opportunities for a writer to work for nothing. From the smallest village magazine to a theatre company with no budget to pay a writer, you will find plenty of outlets. They can provide a reasonable training ground, although some are more useful to an ambitious writer than others.

Your local badminton club may be so desperate for someone to write the newsletter that you'll never get any helpful feedback on your attempts to lighten it with some comedy, whereas your local amateur dramatic group will almost certainly go the other extreme and be very cautious about putting on a production by an unknown writer. In case you were wondering, this is because they usually need to fill the seats to keep the books balanced, and an Alan Ayckbourn play is more likely to do that than yours. You might, however, be able to persuade them to undertake a reading of your play at one of their meetings, so that at least you'd hear it read and get some feedback.

 ## Key idea

At the start of your career, it's worth taking up some of these unpaid opportunities, but try to see them as a stepping stone, not a stopping place.

Freebies

Make a list of all the unpaid ways you could get involved with writing in your local community.

The submissions process

Whether you want to place a sitcom or a novel, certain things are common to all submission processes. At the start of your career, most of your submissions will be cold calling – where you send work out to people and organizations that haven't asked to see it. You have to persuade them that you are talented, reliable and worth investing in. Luckily, everyone is looking for the next big thing, so there will always be a way in for new writers. It isn't easy, though, so you need to do everything you can to improve the odds in your favour.

Focus point

Remember that your day job keeps you in touch with the real world, so use that to your advantage.

In some cases, you'll need to send a proposal (for a drama), a treatment (for a movie) or a synopsis (for a novel), rather than the finished work. In all these cases create something straightforward that explains the proposed work in simple terms. Don't strain to be funny, and don't keep any secrets – even if the piece has a surprise ending, it's only meant to be a surprise for the audience. Demonstrate the quality of your comedy writing by enclosing sample pages from the proposed work. These should be fully polished, not a draft, and give a real flavour of what you're suggesting.

Key idea

Always send your best work.

Write a synopsis

Write a one-page synopsis of the short piece you wrote earlier (for Chapters 10 and 11).

- Summarize it in a sentence of not more than 30 words – be sure to capture the essence of the piece.
- Describe the main elements of the plot.
- As you mention each main character, add the characteristic that drives them forwards.
- Include the setting.
- Add the binding ties if these are not obvious from either the setting or the characters.
- Explain the conflict that will drive the plot forwards.
- Explain the ending.

Always do some research into the organization concerned before you submit. Most of this can be done online, or by consulting directories like *The Writers' & Artists' Yearbook* and *The Writers' Handbook*. There's no point in submitting a comic novel to a publisher that only publishes romance. At best you'll have wasted your time and at worst you'll have created a bad impression that might just have a knock-on effect.

Do some research

Research writing opportunities in your chosen medium and list all the organizations you could submit work to.

Focus point

Many organizations' websites have writers' guidelines – check these and be sure to conform to them.

Make your submission as professional looking as possible. Spell-check your work and then read it through to double-check for mistakes. Lay it out cleanly. Check whether the organization concerned prefers electronic or paper submissions.

If you're posting hard copy, never send handwritten work and always keep a copy or computer backup. Print it out on one side of white A4 paper in black ink. Use a simple font (Arial, Times New Roman or Courier) and 12-point size. Leave wide margins at the top, bottom and sides to allow readers room to make notes. Number the pages and fasten them together in the top left-hand corner – many readers like to take the fastener out and read loose pages, so make it easy for them. The numbering means they can be re-assembled easily if dropped. Include your contact details on the first page.

Don't add anything in the way of photos and drawings and don't have it professionally bound – these are the marks of an amateur. Devise a simple system for record keeping, so that you know where a piece of work has been sent, on what date, and what the result was.

YOUR COVERING LETTER

Include a covering letter (or email). Keep it short – one page is enough. Never start it 'Dear Sir or Madam'. Find out the name of the relevant person, by checking the website or phoning. Keep the letter simple and to the point and don't try to be funny. You only need three paragraphs:

1 Say who you are and describe briefly the work you are submitting or the idea you are proposing.

2 Say briefly why you think your work will be of interest to the audience and what makes it different.

3 Say something about yourself that gives the impression that you are both professional and talented.

 Write a covering letter

Write a three-paragraph covering letter to go with your synopsis.

YOUR CV

Include a CV if you think it's appropriate. Keep it to one page and be sure to include your contact details. Include personal information only if it's relevant to the work concerned. The same applies to your education, hobbies and jobs. Most of the page should be about your writing life. If you're at the start of your career you might feel that there isn't much to say, but include everything you've done. Even if you can't claim anything impressive, it will still show that you take writing seriously and spend time doing it rather than dreaming about doing it. Present yourself in the best possible light (no self-deprecating jokes) but don't on any account tell lies – you'll be found out for sure. Keep the CV short and to the point. Don't use fancy fonts, gimmicky layouts or artwork in the hope of getting noticed – let your writing do that for you.

Write your CV

Write a full CV for yourself. Cover your personal life, your professional life and your writing life. Now reduce it to three one-page versions tailored to accompany:

- a job application
- an application to volunteer with a charity
- a comedy writing submission.

FEEDBACK AND REJECTION

It can take a long time before you get a response. Don't make a nuisance of yourself by asking what's happening to your work. Start writing something else, and if you haven't heard anything in six weeks, send an enquiry.

If you're very lucky, you'll get some feedback when your submission is returned to you. At one time, organizations routinely employed readers to write short reports on unsolicited submissions, but that is fairly rare now. Some writing competitions include feedback on entries, which can be useful.

However the feedback reaches you, you'll need to develop a tough skin and keep an open mind. The tough skin is because some feedback is very cruel. You need the open mind because it's very easy to leap immediately to the defence of your precious work. Try to understand what the feedback is saying, and whether, just possibly, it could be right. Of course, the reader is only one person, you'll know nothing about who they are and whether they have any experience and insight, and you have to bear that in mind, too.

In most instances, all you're going to get is a simple rejection and you're going to have to learn to deal with it. (Dealing with success can be hard, too, but, hopefully, if it happens to you you'll be able to afford an expensive therapist.)

If someone is interested in your work, you may well be invited in for discussions – as a result of which you may be asked to write something entirely different. You may also be asked to sign a release form before any meeting or discussion. This will acknowledge that the ideas behind your work may not be unique and that the organization may well be considering other, similar ideas. You may not like doing this, but you'll have no choice. You will still own the copyright in your words, but there is no copyright in ideas.

Focus point

The simple trick of watching the credits on TV panel shows will tell you whether they are using writers for the material that seems so off-the-cuff. Record programmes so that you can freeze frame to read the credits.

Submissions specifics

Paul Hayes-Watkins, Art Director, *Saga* magazine

'Consider the needs and tone of the title you're contributing to: political, sophisticated, just-for-laughs, senior? If in doubt, ask. Style is also important – would your cartoon (however funny you think it is) sit comfortably next to the magazine's editorial? A great example of this is The New Yorker; *they publish the work of many talented cartoonists but, crucially, the cartoons all look like they "belong".'*

JOKES, CARTOONS AND GREETINGS CARDS

Always submit jokes in batches – at least ten at a time. Twenty would be better. The only exception to this if the BBC has a programme with an open submissions policy, where they will look at everything, even a single joke. At the time of writing, *Newsjack* on Radio 7 was the only open-door programme (see Appendix G, Taking it further).

Stand-up comedians often write their own material at first, but as they become more successful they sometimes need more material than they can generate. Use the Internet to find the name of their agent and make contact that way.

Similarly, when submitting cartoons, send several to show that you have staying power. Number each frame and include an explanation of the visuals if you're sending sketches for another artist to draw.

With greetings cards, check the writers' guidelines for each company and be prepared to send several ideas at a time.

SKETCHES AND SCRIPTS

For sketches submit in batches, although don't overwhelm the reader – send between four and six sketches at a time. Give each sketch a title so that it can be easily identified and use the appropriate script layout – see below for more on this.

For all types of script, make clear distinctions between speeches and instructions such as stage directions. Don't allow speeches to run across two pages and put END at the end of the script.

MOVIES, TV AND RADIO

Movies, TV and radio all have standard formats for laying out a script. The BBC standard layouts can be downloaded from their website (see Appendix G, Taking it further).

If you're sending a proposal, it should summarize the premise in a few words. Go on to say what is special about it, and in particular what will appeal to the audience. Then expand on the idea, giving detail, and provide the answers to any obvious practical and budgetary questions.

Write a proposal

Write a proposal for the full-length piece you mapped out in Chapter 12. (You can do this for a novel as well as a performance piece.)

1. Start with a log line – this is a short plot summary, maybe two sentences or 200 characters.
2. Describe the main characters, starting with the protagonist. Focus on their motivation and flaws.
3. Summarize the main dramatic points of the plot.
4. Say something about the market for the piece.
5. Mention the competition, and say how your piece is different and better.
6. Say a little about yourself as a writer.

If you want to write for radio DJs, start by contacting your local station and offering them your services.

THEATRE

There is no accepted standard layout for theatre scripts, but do make sure that your layout is simple and easily understood. In fact, most scripts follow the layout guidelines listed in the workshop below.

Workshop

Format the stage version of your sketch as follows:

- Create a title page with the name of the sketch, your name and your contact details.
- Create brief descriptions of characters, the set and props.
- Distinguish between speeches and everything else such as the speaker's name and stage directions. Using capitals for everything except speeches is the easiest way to do this.
- Keep the speaker's names on the left-hand side of the page. Some readers like to cover the names and read the speeches alone to see whether they can tell who is speaking (if they can't, it's a black mark).
- Have single-line spacing within speeches and double-line spacing between speeches, and between speeches and stage directions.
- If a direction falls within a speech, put it in brackets as well as in capitals.

JOURNALISM

Most publications have their own writers' guidelines, and these are usually on the website. You should submit either a proposal or a fully finished piece – never send a draft or notes. Always include a word count.

Key idea

While most editors prefer proposals, in the case of comedy they do need to see a sample of your work.

PUBLISHING

Most publishers have submissions guidelines on their websites. As a basic rule, send a synopsis (500 words maximum) and three sample chapters for a novel.

THE INTERNET

There are plenty of websites specifically for writers, and other websites that need written material. Some of these are looking for comedy but very few of them pay. Be sure you understand what you're getting into – in other words, read the small print.

 Key idea

> Once your work is on the Web it's very easily stolen, and even though you own the copyright it can be virtually impossible to keep control of it.

Other factors

AGENTS

For some types of writing, it's possible to work through an agent who will help place work, negotiate fees and so on, in return for a percentage of your earnings. At the beginning of your career, when you most need an agent, it will be difficult to persuade one to take you on, whereas once you're successful it'll be much easier. If you decide to look for an agent, approach them in exactly the same way as you would any other submission.

COPYRIGHT

You automatically own the copyright in everything you write and you don't need to register your copyright, although if you suspect that your work has been stolen you might need to prove when you wrote it. If you work on a computer, that is taken care of by the way documents are dated. However, there is no copyright in ideas, and you'll inevitably find that other writers have had similar ideas to you. In practice, most organizations are honourable and it is very rare to have your copyright abused. (Copyright law is complicated, however, but more detailed information is beyond the scope of this book.)

FOREIGN MARKETS

Those of us who write in English are lucky. Not only is there a large English-speaking community out there, but many countries have English as their second language. Holland and Germany have a long tradition of buying material from English comedy writers. Buyers there and in other countries are happy to arrange translation.

Clearly, you need to remove all wordplay jokes, and all but the most basic of English idioms. It goes without saying that visual comedy sells well in foreign markets.

SHOWREELS

Where there is a performance element to your writing, you may want to send a showreel, either of yourself or of someone performing your work. You can pay to have a professional showreel made, but it is possible to create your own. It is meant to be a sample, so keep it to five minutes or under. Just like any other submission, it should be immaculately presented and include your contact details.

NETWORKING

There are endless opportunities for networking. Unless you live somewhere extraordinarily remote, start with your local community. Join any writers' groups, or maybe start one. Attend workshops and courses, as much for the people you'll meet as anything else. If you're interested in playwriting, visit your local theatre regularly and find out whether they have any writers' schemes. If journalism is your thing, ask the editor of your local paper if they'll take some humorous pieces. You simply never know where these things might lead.

On the Internet, you can join any number of forums and networking sites. Don't let them take over your life, but do try to have a presence. If you can set up your own website then do so; then you can build up traffic by always including a link to it in everything you do.

Ways to network

Research ways you can network in your local community.
Consider:

- theatres and other performances spaces (they often support new writing)
- amateur drama groups
- creative writing groups
- publishers based in your area
- local radio
- local TV
- comedy clubs near you.

You've now reached the end of the final chapter – well done you! However, keep reading: although there are no more exercises there is a wealth of information in the following appendices. Appendix A briefly explores other types of comedy writing, Appendix B looks at comedy styles and genres, and Appendix C shows you how to put your work out there yourself. Appendix D has more information about language. Appendix E lists all the works mentioned in the book and, if you are interested, Appendix F gives you the full texts of my various examples. Finally, Appendix G, Taking it further, lists resources for a comedy writer.

Appendix A:
Other types of
comedy writing

This book has focused very much on writing for performance and writing prose, but there are many other ways to write comedy. Some are simply other outlets for existing work while others are highly specialized forms of writing. However, the basics of comedy writing apply throughout: a joke's a joke; it's how you tell it that varies.

Animation

This is a specialized and complex art form. It includes drawn animation (such as *The Simpsons*), model animation (*Wallace and Gromit*) cut-out animation (*South Park*) and computer animation (*Toy Story*). Computer-generated imagery (CGI) has created a form that includes both real and animated (*The Mask, Who Framed Roger Rabbit?*). Clearly the laws of physics don't apply in animation and characters can be made to do the impossible. Writers have to think visually and characters need to be very strongly defined. Audiences seem to find it easier to engage with very extreme satirical material in animation, perhaps because it is at several removes from reality.

Cartoons

Animated movies are often called cartoons, but here we're looking at strips and single-frame cartoons that you might find in a newspaper or magazine. Surprisingly, you don't need to be able to draw beautifully. You can either devise your own rough-and-ready style or work with an artist.

Paul Hayes-Watkins, Art Director, *Saga* magazine

'*Many of the contributions come into the magazine digitally now, which is perfectly acceptable. However, I would request that once the cartoonist has scanned and prepared their work for despatch... please, please, please don't feel the need to colour the cartoons with the airbrush colouring tool! If the cartoon really needs colour – put it on the traditional way.*'

Remember that we read English from top to bottom and left to right. The drawing part of a cartoon is almost always the equivalent of the set-up to a joke and the text, which is along the bottom, is the punchline. Speech bubbles, however, are usually towards the top, so the reader will absorb them at the same time as they take in the content of the drawing. Have as few words as possible in a frame – 25 is the maximum.

 ## Kev F Sutherland, comedian and comic artist (Beano, Marvel, Viz, etc.)

'In comics, many first-time writers forget there are pictures and don't use them. Talking heads make for very boring comics, and too many words run the risk of it stopping being a comic strip at all. (Some comics writers put in so many words it becomes clear they actually want to write stuff that's not comics.)'

Three- or four-frame cartoons are rather like quickies. If you're creating a series, you'll need sustainable ideas – some cartoons run for decades. There is no character development in that type of cartoon, and the focus is always on the main character – Garfield for instance. The first frame contains the set-up, the next two or three frames develop it and the final frame contains the punchline. Again, be extremely economical with words: dialogue needs to be as short as possible and any captions must be to the point.

Children

Children love to laugh and acquire an instinctive understanding of comedy at an early age. Younger children like silly slapstick humour; older children enjoy joke books but also demand satisfying stories. Avoid sentimentality, satire, sarcasm and irony. Tell the story from the child's point of view. Children like to see the adult world undermined in some way, and they like a strong moral code with the good guys winning in the end. (For more on this, see *Get Started in Writing for Children* and *Complete Writing For Children Course*.)

Greetings cards and e-cards

The market for humorous greetings cards is huge and, once again, you don't have to be able to draw, as companies will buy your ideas and add the artwork (of course, you can expect to earn more if you can also supply the artwork). A humorous card is basically a joke – the front of the card, both words and pictures, is the set-up and the inside of the card is the punchline. It's important to keep cards personal, so use 'I', 'Me' and 'You'.

Pantomime

The world of professional pantomime writing can be extremely difficult to break into, but there is a strong market for scripts for amateur groups. Of course a panto is not a pure comedy and the comedy elements are usually confined to two or three characters. It's a writing challenge: you'll need to include something for the children as well as something for the adults that the children won't understand. As well as jokes arising out of character and plot, you'll need to tack on slapstick and topical jokes. (For more on this, see *Masterclass: Writing Plays*, which has a chapter on panto.)

Poetry

There is a strong humorous element to the current poetry scene, and this is particularly true of performance poetry. However, the whole point of it is that the poet performs their own work. There are also numerous print outlets for poetry, although very few of them are able to pay. (For more on this, see *Write Poetry and Get It Published*, which has a short chapter on performance poetry.)

Radio DJs

There are so many radio stations and each DJ needs material – they have to say something in between the music tracks and there's a particular need for amusing chat on the breakfast-time and drive-time shows, when commuters are listening on car radios.

Songwriting

Comic songwriting is a specialized discipline, but there is always a demand, especially on news-based radio shows like *The Now Show*, where Mitch Benn contributes songs on topical subjects. More often than not, the writer is also the performer. There's also a strong crossover between comedy and music - see performers like Bill Bailey, *The Flight of the Conchords* and *The Mighty Boosh*. If you use existing tunes you need to be aware of copyright issues. (For more on this, see *Get Started in Songwriting*.)

Training and speechwriting

These more specialized disciplines can be interesting and lucrative. Both make use of humour to keep the attention of listeners, and to make hard information more easily absorbed. Politicians often employ separate gag writers to inject some comedy into the material produced by their speechwriters.

Don't expect your clients to have the same skills as professional performers – you'll need to write material that is easy for them to put across. Meet them if possible, so that you get a feel for how they talk naturally, and do everything you can to persuade them to rehearse.

Merchandise: T-shirts, bumper stickers and mugs

All of these use jokes and manufacturers will pay for them.

Appendix B: Comedy styles and genres

There are many different ways of making people laugh, and comedy can be divided in various ways into styles and genres. They tend to overlap and most comedy falls into more than one category. In the same way, writers and performers will often work with more than one type of comedy. You will already have your own preferences and an instinct for the type of comedy you want to write, but an understanding of the different categories will help you when you're trying to place your work.

Types of comedy

Alternative comedy

This usually refers specifically to the comedy of the 1980s, which was more political than the mainstream comedy of the time and wasn't joke based.

Black comedy

Black comedy deals with difficult and disturbing subjects such as death and war. *The League of Gentlemen* and *Psychoville* are recent TV examples that aim to make you laugh while simultaneously sending a shiver down your spine. Some black comedy has a deeply serious aim, for instance Kurt Vonnegut's anti-war novel *Slaughterhouse 5*.

Blue comedy

This term comes from the music-hall comedian Max Miller, who kept all his naughty jokes in a blue notebook. It mostly refers to jokes about sex and bodily functions, but can also include profanity, swearing and anything else likely to shock that particular audience. Live performance is always far more extreme than TV, movie or radio. Some performers have two acts, keeping the bluer one for their live appearances, while others, like Jethro and Roy 'Chubby' Brown, confine themselves to live work.

Burlesque

Burlesque is a form of theatrical comedy which started as a combination of sexual come-on and parody of opera and classical theatre. In the buttoned-up Victorian era the scantily dressed women offered audiences something truly exciting, and burlesque challenged mainstream standards. It was hugely popular as a result but disappeared in the late twentieth century. Recently there's been something of a revival, although burlesque no longer offers a titillating contrast with the mainstream.

Caricature and impressions

Both of these involve picking up on the traits of a real, well-known person and exaggerating them to get laughs. Caricatures are more extreme and less realistic than impressions. Satirists use both to make serious points.

Character comedy

Just as it sounds, character comedy derives humour from the characters' behaviours and reactions. It is the driving force of sitcom and much other comedy.

Crossover

Crossover takes characters from one comedy and moves them into another. Frasier Crane was a minor character in *Cheers* but was moved into *Frasier* as the main character. Characters can also make occasional appearances: Sam Malone, the central character from *Cheers* was written into one episode of *Frasier*. The term crossover is sometimes mistakenly used to describe comedy drama.

Deadpan

As mentioned in Chapter 7, deadpan comedians keep a straight face whatever happens.

High and low comedy

These rather old-fashioned terms still have some relevance, because there is still a certain amount of snobbery that tends to discount low comedy. Low comedy includes most physical comedy, silly jokes, horseplay and so on. High comedy is more cerebral, although it's worth noting that to be successful it often needs to include elements of low comedy: *Monty Python's Flying Circus* is a good example of this.

Improvisational comedy

Mike Leigh has been using improvisation to create scripts since the 1970s. In recent years, stand-up comedians have developed an improv approach, starting in comedy clubs and then moving into TV via radio. Initially only short pieces were improvised, for instance in the 1980s show *Whose Line Is It Anyway?* Recently there have been improvised sitcoms, including the US show *Curb Your Enthusiasm* and the UK's *Getting On*. Inevitably the performers also get the writing credits.

Irony

See Appendix D, Figures of speech.

Mockumentary

This portmanteau word means 'mock documentary'. It's a type of parody and is currently popular in TV and movie comedy. The key is to use the conventions of the documentary form but undermine them in some way. For instance, *The Office* creates an entire fictional world in the style of a documentary, whereas Sacha Baron Cohen takes his fictional characters out into the real world.

Music-based comedy

This covers a wide range of possibilities, including parodies of popular songs, new lyrics for old songs and so on. It is not to be confused with musical comedy, a theatre genre that is entertaining but not usually funny.

Observational comedy

See Chapter 6.

Parody

Parody is also called send-up, spoof or lampoon. The aim is to take an established piece of work or a performance and create a new version that highlights and exaggerates its features to the point of absurdity. Impressionists inevitably use parody related to the subject of the impression.

It goes without saying that the target of the parody needs to be well known to the audience. When Jane Austen parodied Gothic novels in her early novel *Northanger Abbey,* she was picking on a popular format. Being the subject of parody could be seen as a mark of success.

Satire

Satire aims to point out the shortcomings of society, organizations and individuals by ridiculing them. Satirical writers often have a desire to force change, and so it is comedy with a purpose, and often quite short-lived because of its topical nature. However, some satire survives, for instance Aldous Huxley's *Brave New World*.

Irony, parody and sarcasm are all useful tools of the satirist's trade. Panel shows such as *The News Quiz* on Radio 4 and *Have I Got News For You* on BBC TV are predominantly satirical.

If you're writing satire, you need a strongly developed sense of how far to go. It's easy to alienate an audience by overdoing the satire – the last thing you want is to create sympathy for your target. Equally, you need to be sure the audience will understand that you're being satirical. In 2001 the 'Paedophile Special' of the series *Brass Eye* caused uproar because it arguably missed its target, which was supposed to be the media stoking a culture of fear towards paedophiles through witchhunts.

Political satire uses comedy with serious intent but the prime requirement for it is to be funny. As Peter Cook pointed out, the fashion for satire in 1930s Berlin had little effect on the rise of Hitler.

Slapstick

Slapstick is a type of physical comedy involving cartoon-like violence and extreme behaviours. It's been around for a very long time but we never seem to tire of it. Charlie Chaplin and Buster Keaton took slapstick into the movies and many comedy movies are still essentially slapstick: *Airplane, Spaceballs, Ace Ventura Pet Detective, Mask, Home Alone, Naked Gun* and so on.

Surreal comedy

Surreal comedy is connected to the surrealist movement in art but actually predates it, since Lewis Carroll's humour is surreal. Surreal comedy is bizarre and absurd, but there is still a degree of internal logic. *The Goon Show* was the first popular surreal comedy, and *Monty Python* brought the genre to TV. More recently, *The Mighty Boosh* is carrying on the tradition. It's difficult to write unless you have a natural tendency in that direction, and most of the writers are also performers.

Topical comedy

Doing exactly what it says on the tin, topical comedy relies on news and current affairs as its source material. Writers have to be quick off the mark and get the material out there while the news items are still hot.

Comedy genres

Comedy drama

Comedy drama mixes comedy with drama in roughly equal proportions. Some people feel that trying to do two things means you end up doing neither of them well, but there is a sizable audience for it. When it is done well, the drama element drives the plot forward while the comedy keeps the audience entertained. Theatre and movie comedy dramas tend to be one-off stories, while on TV they are more likely to be a filmed series. At one time this would consist of a story told over several episodes (such as *The Beiderbecke Trilogy*) but recently US TV companies have found a winning formula for ongoing soap-opera type comedy dramas such as *Glee, Desperate Housewives* and *Ugly Betty*.

Comedy of manners

This is a form of satire that focuses on the affectations of a particular social class. Although its heyday was in the seventeenth century, Oscar Wilde and Noël Coward continued the tradition. Witty dialogue is essential, along with a plot that revolves round breaking a social taboo.

Comedy thriller

This is a popular movie and novel genre that's been around for a while – the classic *The Thin Man* was made in 1934. Usually these movies are action-based and avoid the graphic violence of many straight thrillers, but not always – *Grosse Point Blank* utilized comedy values but is about a cold-blooded killer. Carl Hiaasen combines comedy thrillers with environmental concerns in his novels.

Farce

Farce started as a theatre genre characterized by a fast-moving plot full of unlikely situations, misunderstandings, disguises and hidden agendas. Usually there is a central protagonist with something to hide and the plot hinges on their increasing desperation. There is usually a happy ending, although this isn't obligatory. It has been unpopular in recent years and is seen as rather unsophisticated. However, elements of farce appear in many sitcoms, movies and stage plays.

Romantic comedy

Romantic comedy, or romcom, is a genre in which two apparently unsuited people are eventually united for a happy ending. Jane Austen is the first romcom novelist. Movie examples are *It Happened One Night* (1924) and *Love Actually* (2003). TV series such as *Ugly Betty* and *Gavin and Stacey* use the same conventions but rarely reach an entirely happy ending since the makers are generally hoping for another series.

Tragicomedy

This is a serious piece that uses comedy to lighten the mood or to throw the sad aspects of the story into sharp contrast. There doesn't necessarily have to be a happy ending, and tragicomedy lends itself to a mixed or ironic ending. Alan Ayckbourn and Mike Leigh have both specialized in tragicomedies.

Appendix C:
Doing it yourself

If your work has been rejected, and you have faith in it, then you could think of going it alone. Rejection can be for all sorts of reasons apart from poor quality. Organizations have limited budgets for a start, or they might already have committed to something that is too similar to your work.

DIY – common ground

The main advantage of getting your work in front of an audience is the simple pleasure it will give you. It's immensely fulfilling to hear a group of people laughing at your jokes, or to have someone say how much they enjoyed your novel.

Of course there are difficulties. The main one is that it will be a lot of work, and most of that work isn't writing. Instead of writing comedy, the one thing you really want to do, you'll be getting your head round print runs or actors' insurance, or how the camcorder works. This all takes time and energy, both of which you'd probably rather devote to writing.

Getting feedback

You can get feedback on your work in various ways – from the audience, from reviews, from anyone involved in the production process. You can seek it out, for instance by including a questionnaire in a theatre programme or an email address in a book. However it arrives, take note of it and use it to improve your writing. In fact, always do a rewrite where possible – after a performance, for instance. It's not possible to rewrite a novel once it's published, but you can learn lessons for the next one.

Marketing

Most of us don't have the skills or resources for publicity and marketing, and yet these are absolutely vital to any DIY effort. You can't build a career on the sales you make to your friends and family.

For most forms of DIY, marketing is the biggest difficulty. Unless you already have fantastic contacts in the media, it is going to be hard work. Write a sparkling press release and send it to all your local publications, and any national ones that you think might be interested. Also send it to local TV and radio stations. Include a review copy if your work is a book, and free tickets if it's a performance. Offer to talk about your work to local clubs, and take along copies or tickets to sell. Think laterally, and do whatever you can to push your work in front of the public.

You can use your DIY comedy project as a marketing tool for your future career. Make sure it reaches the industry professionals – send them free tickets or free copies of books and recordings. If it is successful, you can use it as a stepping stone into the industry.

Finances

Another big difficulty is cost. You'll have to pay all the costs up front, with no guarantee of getting your money back. In fact you're almost certain to make a loss, so it's best to write that money off from the start. Always establish what the costs will be before you commit yourself to a project. Make a list of everything you'll need to pay for and add a contingency fund.

DIY specifics

Stand-up routines

If you're an eccentric millionaire, then by all means start your own comedy club. Otherwise, the DIY route with jokes is to get involved with your local open-mic night, either at a club or a pub. The normal set for these nights is three to five minutes – check with the venue. In fact, visit the venue as an audience member first. Familiarize yourself with the set-up and get to know the staff, if possible.

If you are really determined not to perform yourself, you'll need a friend who has performing ambitions or who at least enjoys performing. Whoever is performing, be sure to rehearse the act and try it out in front of a few willing victims beforehand. On the night, arrive early and remind yourself that the audience are there to enjoy themselves – they'll want to meet you halfway. However well it's going, a comic should get off in good time – it's always best to leave them wanting more. Make friends with the other performers and be supportive towards them rather than critical – they may want to buy your material one day.

(For more about stand-up, see *Get Started in Stand-Up Comedy.*)

Greetings cards

If you find it easy to write jokey greetings for special occasions, it's comparatively simple to start a small card business. Obviously, you'll need access to good artwork that captures the mood of the moment. Research what's around by browsing in your local card shop. You'll also need to find a competent printer, since not all of them can manage high-quality colour printing. The easiest way to market cards is to ask local shops to take a few on a sale or return basis, but you could also take a stall at local markets or go to car boot sales.

Theatre

You can put on a production of your own play, or a review if you want to showcase your sketches. Start by deciding who is going to direct, because they'll choose the actors. Finding the people you need is where networking really comes in useful. Use all your contacts to find resting professionals or talented amateurs. Drama students are often interested in gaining experience on small projects, so make contact with local educational establishments. They may also be able to help you find a lighting person, a sound person and set and costume designers. You'll need a backstage crew, front of house, and people to help with setting up and clearing out. That adds up to quite a few people. If you struggle to find people willing to put effort into your play or review, then perhaps it isn't good enough yet and needs a rewrite.

Once you've got the people in place, there's still more to do:

- You'll need a venue – there are plenty of small halls and pub theatres to choose from.
- You'll also need a separate rehearsal space – your living room won't be big enough.
- Don't forget insurance. Find out what insurance the venue has and top it up if necessary.
- You'll need to create programmes and tickets – use the programme as a publicity opportunity for everyone involved. Include a number and email address for the box office. It's unlikely the venue will do this so you'll probably end up selling the tickets yourself.
- Use the artwork from the programme to create flyers, which you can spread around the local area to publicize the performances.
- It's worth videoing a performance to help you with the inevitable rewrite. The quality won't be good enough to send out professionally, but it will mean you have a record.

For more on this, see *Write a play and get it performed* or *Make Your Show a Success*.

When Ann Gawthorpe and I put on a small professional production of our play *Over Exposure,* we both worked on it full time for three months. It really does need that many hours of input to do it properly

TV, radio and movies

No, unfortunately you can't just set up your own TV or radio station (yes, I know there are pirate stations out there, but you're on your own with that one). You can, however, record your work and send it out to production companies, or post it on the Internet. You'll need the appropriate equipment and a reasonable level of technical competence. You can perform your own work if it is a solo effort. Otherwise go through the process of finding a director, actors and a crew.

There is no legal reason why you shouldn't set up your own independent movie company (known as an Indie) but the most likely way to showcase your work for film is to make a short and enter it for competitions. You'll need a cast and crew for anything other than a video of you doing stand-up so, just as with theatre, you'll need to network, and track down students of filmmaking. (For more on this, see *Get Started in Film Making*.)

Journalism and cartoons

If you can't find an outlet for your humorous journalism and cartoons, consider starting your own magazine or comic. Magazines for adults generally rely on advertising to achieve financial balance and somebody has to sell the space – which involves a lot of cold calling and salesmanship. You'll also need to have the magazines printed, since home printers are not up to the job, and a means of distribution.

You'll need to keep up a steady flow of material, unless you offer space to other comedy writers. Cartoons, of course, will need drawing, so if you're only good at the words you'll need to buddy up with an artist.

(For more on this, see *Get your articles published*, which has a chapter on starting your own magazine.)

Self-publishing a novel or joke book

It's perfectly possible to publish your own comedy book. There are plenty of small printers and bookbinders who will produce the book for you. You'll need a cover design, something eye-catching and stylish, and there will be decisions to make about font, page layout and margins. You'll be responsible for editing and proofreading, but both these tasks are best carried out by someone else, who comes to the book fresh. You'll need somewhere to store the copies and above all you'll need to market the book.

If you are hoping to place the book in bookshops, it will need an International Standard Book Number, and this will also enable you to sell it on Amazon through their Advantage scheme.

Some companies will publish your book for you – for a fee of course. It's very important to distinguish between companies that genuinely help you publish and those that offer what is known as vanity publishing, where you pay a great deal of money for a few fancy copies of your book.

You can also use an Internet tool, such as Createspace or Lulu, to publish a book. (There is more on this in *Get Your Book Published*.)

The Internet

Most forms of writing can be posted on the Internet. You can write for a blog, on Twitter or on your own website. You can upload songs and videos to YouTube, metacafe or one of the many alternatives. As long as you've got Internet access the cost is minimal – the real challenge is to build a following. The American comedian Bo Burnham started his career on YouTube, so it can be done.

The Edinburgh Fringe

The Edinburgh Fringe is hugely important to the world of comedy. The publicity tends to focus on stand-up performers and the competition to win the annual award for stand-up, but there is a lot more to it than that.

The first key thing to understand about the Edinburgh Fringe is that anyone can take a show there. Most Festivals have a Creative Director who chooses who will appear, but for three weeks in August anyone can make their mark in Edinburgh as long as they can find the money to pay for a venue. The second key thing is that vast numbers of powerful people in the world of entertainment, most of whom are London based, decamp to Edinburgh for the Festival. It is the one place where dreams might come true, and there really might be someone in the audience for your show who can change your life.

Of course it is heavily performance oriented, and writers have to either turn themselves into performers or find people who will make their work come alive.

The best way to go about this is to spend a few days at the Festival one summer, with a view to taking a show there the following summer. You'll get a feel for the smaller venues, which are the only ones most of us can afford. You'll see what hard work it is, and learn from other peoples' mistakes. Then you'll have a whole year to organize your show, and believe me you'll need it.

Appendix D: Figures of speech

The various ways of using language known as figures of speech can almost all be used to create comedy. Remember that word-play jokes on their own usually raise no more than a smile, but they have their place and can add texture to comedy writing.

There are too many figures of speech to list all of them, so here are a few of the most useful (and don't worry if the names are unfamiliar: I had to look them up too).

Alliteration

This is using the same initial letter for a series of words, as used in tongue twisters. If you're writing scripts, be careful not to include accidental tongue twisters that actors might struggle to cope with, although anything sayable might generate a laugh. Here's Adam trying to fit in a client:

> Wendy, check if I've got a window on Wednesday.

Anthropomorphism and zoomorphism

Anthropomorphism means describing animals in human terms. There is a lot of fun to be had out of the person who claims that a particularly dumb pet dog 'understands every word you say' and a somewhat crueller laugh to be had if they say that about another person. Zoomorphism means describing humans in animal terms, for example 'as strong as an ox'.

Euphemism

This is using an acceptable term instead of one that might be considered too blunt or offensive. Most euphemisms are, understandably enough, around sex and bodily functions. There are many ways to use them to get laughs including the very old but still roadworthy trick of decoding the truth behind adverts and jargon. For instance, here is part of a list decoding job advert euphemisms:

> *Apply in person*: if you're old, fat or ugly, you'll be told the position has been filled.
> *Competitive salary*: we remain competitive by paying less than our competitors.
> *Duties will vary*: anyone in the office can boss you around.
> *Join our fast-paced company*: we have no time to train you.
> *Must have an eye for detail*: we have no quality control.

Seeking candidates with a wide variety of experience: you'll need it to replace the three people who just left.

Homonyms and homophones

Homonyms share the same spelling and pronunciation, whereas homophones sound the same but have different spelling and are used to create puns (see below). Clearly, how you use them will depend on whether you're writing for the page or for performance. One can imagine having fun with the words carrot and carat, mixing up vegetables and diamond rings, but only in performance. An extension of this principle using more than one word led to the classic *Two Ronnies* fork handles/four candles sketch.

Irony and sarcasm

Essentially, irony is saying one thing while meaning another, and so is closely linked to sarcasm. Both are comedy staples. They are often conveyed by tone of voice, so if someone is asked to help with the housework, and they reply 'Oh, yes, I'd love to help', there is no way of knowing whether they are being sarcastic unless there is an indication in the text. Their meaning is crystal clear, however, if they say 'Oh, yes, I'd love to help, just about as much as I'd love to jump into a vat of boiling tar.'

The speaker here is being intentionally ironic, but another type of irony occurs when the speaker is unaware of the irony behind their words. So they might offer to help with the housework, not realizing that the house in question has just burned down.

Litotes

Litotes is the odd trick of creating a positive statement by using negatives, such as 'I'm not entirely convinced you're right about that' as a way of saying 'I think you're wrong.'

Pathetic fallacy

This is giving human characteristics to inanimate objects. In literature this usually refers to nature, so that, for instance, characters imagine the weather reflects their mood. To make this funny, it needs to be very obviously inappropriate, for instance when Basil Fawlty loses his temper with his car, addresses it as 'you' and says he's going to give it 'a damn good thrashing'.

Puns

A pun is a play on words. It can be based on a word that has more than one meaning:

The duck said to the bartender, 'Put it on my bill'.

or different words that have the same pronunciation:

Seven days without food make one weak (one week).

The concept can be extended to two or more words:

It is better to have loved a short person and lost, than never to have loved a tall.

Metonymy and synecdoche

Metonymy means using an associated word rather than the actual name of something. For instance, journalists will often use 'Whitehall' to stand for the Civil Service and car drivers will say 'I broke down' when they mean that the car broke down. Synecdoche means using the name of a part of something to refer to the whole thing, such as when workers are called 'hands', and also using the whole of something to refer to the part, such as 'the whole world was against him', meaning that just a part of the world was against him. Dickens uses synecdoche to humorous effect in *Hard Times*:

Lady Scadgers (an immensely fat old woman, with an inordinate appetite for butcher's meat, and a mysterious leg which had now refused to get out of bed for fourteen years)...

Synonyms and antonyms

Synonyms are words that mean the same thing, although usually there is a subtle difference in meaning. If a word has more than one meaning it's likely to have more than one synonym – for instance, *lie* can mean *deceive, recline* or *be located*. Antonyms are opposites, or near opposites, and again the more meanings a word has the more antonyms it will have. Moving between the meanings is a simple way of surprising an audience.

Zeugma and syllepsis

Zeugma is using one verb for two actions:

He kissed her on her forehead, she on his cheek.

Syllepsis is similar, but the two actions are not compatible, and therefore funnier:

She walked out of the house and into his heart.

Clearly, the more incongruous the two actions appear, the funnier the effect.

Appendix E: Works mentioned

Books

Birdsong, Sebastian Faulks

Brave New World, Aldous Huxley

Catch 22, Joseph Heller

David Copperfield, Charles Dickens

Dombey and Son, Charles Dickens

Going Through the Motions, Lesley Bown

Gulliver's Travels, Jonathan Swift

Hard Times, Charles Dickens

Indecent Exposure, Tom Sharpe

Ladies of Letters, Carol Hayman and Lou Wakefield

Lady Chatterley's Lover, D.H. Lawrence

Lord Emsworth Acts for the Best, P.G. Wodehouse

Northanger Abbey, Jane Austen

Pride and Prejudice, Jane Austen

Riotous Assembly, Tom Sharpe

Scenes from a Poisoner's Life, Nigel Williams

Slaughterhouse-Five, Kurt Vonnegut

The Card, Arnold Bennet

The Diary of a Nobody, George and Weedon Grossmith

The Finkler Question, Howard Jacobson

The Inimitable Jeeves, P.G. Wodehouse

The Queen and I, Sue Townsend

The Secret Diary of Adrian Mole, aged 13¾, Sue Townsend

The Timewaster Diaries, Robin Cooper

The Wimbledon Poisoner, Nigel Williams

Ulysses, James Joyce

Films

Ace Ventura Pet Detective

Airplane!

Dr Strangelove or: How I Learned to Stop Worrying and Love the Bomb

Four Weddings and a Funeral

Grosse Point Blank

It Happened One Night

Liar Liar

Little Miss Sunshine

Love Actually

Mamma Mia!

Men in Black

Mr Bean

Mrs Doubtfire

Notting Hill

Shaun of the Dead

Some Like It Hot

The Beverly Hillbillies

The Big Lebowski

The Italian Job

The Mask

The Odd Couple

The Thin Man

The Truman Show

Toy Story

Who Framed Roger Rabbit?

Radio

Newsjack

The Goon Show, Spike Milligan and others

The News Quiz

The Now Show

The Wordsmiths at Gorsemere, Sue Limb

Theatre

Absurd Person Singular, Alan Ayckbourn

Charley's Aunt, Brandon Thomas

The Importance of Being Earnest, Oscar Wilde

The Rivals, Richard Brinsley Sheridan
Who's Afraid of Virginia Woolf? Edward Albee

TV

'Allo 'Allo! David Croft, Jeremy Lloyd, Paul Adam
Absolutely Fabulous, Jennifer Saunders
Black Books, Dylan Moran, Graham Linehan
Blackadder, Richard Curtis, Rowan Atkinson, Ben Elton
Bottom, Adrian Edmonson, Rik Mayall
Brass Eye, Chris Morris, David Quantick, Peter Baynham, Jane Bussmann, Arthur Mathews, Graham Linehan
Cheers, James Burrows, Glen Charles, Les Charles
Christmas Lights, Jeff Pope, Bob Mills
Citizen Smith, John Sullivan
Coupling, Steven Moffat
Curb Your Enthusiasm, Larry David
Desperate Housewives, created by Marc Cherry
Father Ted, Arthur Mathews, Graham Linehan
Fawlty Towers, John Cleese, Connie Booth
Frasier, created by David Angell, Peter Casey, David Lee
Friends, created by David Crane, Marta Kauffman
Gavin and Stacey, James Corden, Ruth Jones
Getting On, created by Jo Brand, Vicki Pepperdine, Joanna Scanlon
Glee, Ryan Murphy, Brad Falchuk, Ian Brennan
Have I Got News For You, panel game show
Home To Roost, Eric Chappell
Keeping Up Appearances, Roy Clarke
Last of the Summer Wine, Roy Clarke
Men Behaving Badly, Simon Nye
Miranda, Miranda Hart
Monty Python's Flying Circus, Graham Chapman, John Cleese, Terry Gilliam, Eric Idle, Terry Jones, Michael Palin
My Family, created by Fred Barron
My Name is Earl, created by Greg Garcia
My Wife Next Door, Brian Clemens, Richard Waring
Nighty Night, Julia Davis

One Foot in the Grave, David Renwick

Only Fools and Horses, John Sullivan

Outnumbered, Guy Jenkin, Andy Hamilton

Porridge, Dick Clement, Ian La Frenais

Red Dwarf, Rob Grant, Doug Naylor

Roseanne, created by Roseanne Barr, Matt Williams

Some Mothers Do 'Ave 'Em, Raymond Allen

South Park, created by Trey Parker

Steptoe and Son, Ray Galton, Alan Simpson

Teenage Kicks, created by Adrian Edmonson, Nigel Smith

The Beiderbecke Trilogy, Alan Plater

The Fast Show, created by Paul Whitehouse, Charlie Higson

The Good Life, Bob Larbey

The IT Crowd, Graham Linehan

The League of Gentlemen, Jeremy Dyson, Mark Gatiss, Steve Pemberton, Reece Shearsmith

The Might Boosh, Julian Barratt, Noel Fielding

The Office, Ricky Gervais, Stephen Merchant

The Royle Family, Craig Cash, Caroline Ahearne

The Simpsons, created by Matt Groening

The Thick Of It, created by Armando Ianucci

The Vicar of Dibley, created by Richard Curtis, Paul Mayhew Archer

Till Death Us Do Part, Johnny Speight

Two Pints of Lager and a Packet of Crisps, Susan Nickson

Ugly Betty, created by Fernando Gaitàn

Wallace and Gromit, created by Nick Park

Whose Line Is It Anyway? Dan Patterson, Mark Leveson

Yes Minister, Antony Jay, Jonathan Lynn

Appendix F: Full texts of examples

Observational stand-up – Chapter 6

LADIES AND GENTLEMEN, WE APOLOGISE FOR THE DELAY...

The cleaning lady enters, with mop and bucket.

I know you're waiting for the bloke what juggles with vibrators, but one of 'em's gone missing so, they've asked me to fill in. I don't why because I'm only the cleaner, but it turns out the singer's got a sore throat and the comedian won't come out of the loo. Men, eh!

I've got nothing against men, mind, but I seen in the papers, them scientists has worked out that men can only do one thing at a time while women, right, women are what's called multifunctional.

Now what that means is a woman can cook the breakfast, delouse the dog, change the spark plug on the motor mower and do the kids' homework all at the same time. But men can only do one thing. And if he's scratching his head, well don't expect him to do nothing else. Blimey, we didn't need no scientist to tell us that, did we? I think we'd worked that one out, hadn't we, girls?

And I don't want to go on about sex, I leave that to the Women's Institute, but you know what it's like don't you, you've got the man shouting, 'Yes yes!' while the woman is getting on with her orgasm, writing a shopping list, and trying to decide whether to go to Venice or Venezuela for next year's holiday. Oh, and if it's Monday morning she's probably changing the sheets and if it's Saturday she'll be stripping the wallpaper off with a chisel, ready to start decorating.

And talking of chisels – don't men ever go mad if you use one instead of a screwdriver? I mean what's the big deal – they look the same, don't they? Anyway, I was only scraping out the oven, no call for him making all that fuss.

'Course, he still thinks that sort of thing is woman's work, along with hoovering, gardening and servicing the car. So don't give me all that New Man stuff. He says he done his bit when he wrote the cheque for the dishwasher. So why is it that as fast as I put the plates in he takes them out again and just ever so slightly rearranges them? What's that all about, then?

Of course, we're told it's all in the genes. I seen on the Internet that them scientists have mapped the genome. I can see you're surprised I use the Internet. Well, I am one of them silver sufferers. You see, it's us women what are into this hands-on technology. Men buy the computers, right, and they boast about the size of their rams and hard drives or whatever, but it's us women what work out how to use 'em. I tell you, I roar down that information superhighway so fast it's a wonder I haven't been booked for speeding.

But back to the genes. Well I'm not no scientist but I could have identified one for them. It's that one what men share with animals. You know like when dogs meet up? No, not that one, come on, let's keep it clean.

No, it's the one with the urinals, right? Can you ever get a man to go past a urinal, no you can't. They've only got to see the magic word 'gents' and they're in there, leaving you standing outside looking like a lemon. I mean, they don't really want to go. They can't want to go. They've been in every urinal since you've left home, there can't be nothing left. No, what they're doing, right, is they are marking territory, just like animals do. Each little splash on some broken filthy bit of porcelain says, 'This is mine, I was here'. And if they can't find a gents, a large tree will do.

But I never say nothing. Live and let live, that's what I say. 'Course, he doesn't see it that way. I says to him, I put up with your urinals, the least you can do is put up with my knickers. When we packs for a holiday we counts them out, don't we girls? One for every day we're away, and a spare pair to carry in our handbags in case the luggage goes to Australia instead of Austria.

But what if we haven't got enough pairs? No problem, we'll wash some out while we're away, won't we? So we just pop in our handbag a washing line, two dozen clothes pegs, a large packet of soap powder, fabric softener, a travelling iron and a bottle of distilled water. I tell you my handbag has often weighed more than my suitcase. Then we spend every morning hand washing everything we wore the day before just to be on the safe side. Well, it's compulsive isn't? The washing dries so well out there.

The old man's hammering on the bathroom door, wanting to know when we're going down the beach. But we ignores him because we knows this is just a code for saying, 'I want to mark territory in every foreign urinal I can', so we carries on buffing up the underwear with a nail brush. One holiday I come home with a suitcase full of clean clothes. I didn't see much of Marbella, but I can always look at his photographs. Mostly urinals, of course.

His proud boast is that he is multilingual and he's right, he knows the word for gents in seventeen languages, although when he thinks we are going to visit Outer Mongolia is anybody's guess.

Still, it's good for men to have a hobby isn't it, and at least his doesn't cost any money. And why is that? Why do women have to pay and not men? It's one of those strange facts of life such as bread always falling butter-side down even when you're using Flora.

Hang on a minute, I can see the juggler's waving a vibrator over his head. So here's the act you've been waiting for...

Character voice – Chapter 7

SAVING MONEY IN THESE STRAITENED TIMES

The credit crunch has hit all of us terribly hard, but I put on the old thinking cap and, as usual, I came up with a simply brilliant idea. It came to me in a flash - instead of popping across to Tuscany as per usual, we would buy a 'motorized caravan' and save absolutely heaps of money. Bertie and I took our first trip over the Bank Holiday and had a perfectly splendid time. If you, too, are thinking of joining the merry band of motoring caravanners, then here are a few little tips.

Firstly, there is no need to go to all the trouble and expense of procuring hothouse lilies, (although by all means, if the gardener is able to provide them, you may as well enjoy their scent). But a few blooms from the rose garden in a simple cut-glass vase will provide an elegant focal point for your living area. I designed a shelf to fit in the gap between the washroom wall and the TV cupboard.

Making the shelf was perfectly simple – there is a little man in the village who does all that sort of thing for one, and of course his wife is quite capable of making the new velvet curtains with swags and pelmets to replace the rather mean window dressings supplied with the camping van. While she had the Singer out, it took very little extra effort for her to add the finishing touches to the four-poster that her husband had cleverly inserted into the space previously occupied by the very inadequate bed arrangement.

Do not, of course, pack the best china. The Sèvres dinner service is hardly appropriate and you can 'rough it' perfectly well with the second-best Royal Worcester. One little tip that is well worth remembering is that grandma's silver teapot is unbreakable and ideal for a camping 'brew-up', as I believe it's called.

However many berths one has in one's motoring caravan, it is simply foolish to allow the butler to use one of them. The thing to do is to send the man on ahead with a pup tent, which will be quite adequate for his needs. With judicious planning, it should be possible for him to serve one's breakfast at home and be on the camping site ready with luncheon just as one arrives.

And finally, do not waste part of your precious payload carrying logs, kindling and firelighters. Try as you might, you won't find a fireplace anywhere in a motor caravanette – something of an oversight that I intend to write to the manufacturers about. Poor Bertie had to stick his feet under the grill to achieve his favourite toasty warm sensation in his lower limbs.

I think you'll find that if you follow my advice you'll have a perfectly charming time in your van without spending a fortune, and still manage to live in the style to which we are all accustomed. However, I don't recommend staying away from home for too long – after a week without fingerbowls, even the strongest among us begins to quail.

Sketch – Chapter 8
FUNERAL FUN

A woman enters a funeral parlour.

Undertaker: May one be of assistance?

Woman: Um… yes… it's a bit awkward.

Undertaker: Modom has come to make arrangements for the dear departed? Rest assured, we are professionals.

Woman: No, no, it's not that…

Undertaker: Modom is aware that this is a funeral parlour?

Woman: (*Angry*) Is it? Are you sure? (*Makes an effort at self-control. Produces a piece of paper*). Actually it's about this bill of yours…

Undertaker: (*Taking the bill from her*) Ah, yes. Funeral of Mr Johnson. I take it Modom is here on behalf of Mrs Johnson?

Woman: Yes. She's my aunt. (*Beat*) It is a lot of money.

Undertaker: Mrs Johnson requested our top-of-the-range funeral. The Jeeves.

Woman: Yes. You see, she is rather elderly. I'm not sure that she entirely understood the, er, the implications.

Undertaker: And then there is the extra charge for the services of the embalmer. Did you view the deceased in our Chapel of Jest?

Woman: Yes. Quite a shock.

Undertaker: So very lifelike. One almost expects the deceased to leap out of the coffin…

Woman: …and say 'Mr Grimsdale!'

Undertaker: Ah yes, you had the Norman Wisdom. Very impressive.

Woman: Considering my uncle was six foot three and sixteen stone.

Undertaker: A triumph of the embalmer's art. Only possible when expense is no object.

Woman: It certainly wasn't cheap. And did we really need two priests for the service?

Undertaker: That is standard with the Jeeves. (*Woman looks puzzled*) For the dead parrot sketch at the altar? (*Does a bad imitation of John Cleese*) 'This is an ex-parrot'?

Woman: (*Not amused*) Yes. I was there. I think we'd have preferred it without the, er, frills.

Undertaker: Is Modom referring to our basic funeral, the Coco? It lacks the richness of the Jeeves, but the priest does wear a red nose and a revolving bow tie instead of his dog collar. A little obvious, perhaps, but most effective for a certain class of person.

Woman: It's just that it's not what we were expecting.

Undertaker: No? Surely Mrs Johnson understood the nature of our service to the bereaved? (*He reveals a poster on the wall that reads 'We put the FUN back in FUNERAL'*)

Woman: My aunt just wanted to do the best for her husband.

Undertaker: Quite so, Modom. The Jeeves was clearly the most suitable. Everything of the best. Finest mahogany coffin, very solid...

Woman: ...that's true. The poor chap had quite a struggle to saw it in half. (*She takes out her credit cards*) Look, I just want to pay the bill and forget about the whole thing. How much altogether?

Undertaker: That all depends on Modom's final decision. Regarding the ashes? (*He produces three identical urns from beneath the counter.*)

Woman: Which one is it?

Undertaker: That one. (*He takes the lid off, shows her the ashes, replaces the lid.*) Keep your eye on it. (*He swaps them round rapidly.*) Choose one.

Woman: Er... that one?

Undertaker: Sure?

Woman: Yes. No. Oh, that one. (*She opens an urn. A boxing glove on a spring pops out.*)

Undertaker: Modom wasn't paying attention, was Modom? It's this one, of course. (*He gives her the correct urn.*) We can arrange disposal if required.

Woman: (*Clutching the urn protectively*) I don't want my uncle turned into sneezing powder!

Undertaker: Ah, very funny, Modom. I'm afraid the ashes of deceased persons would never meet the required standard for sneezing powder. We merely place the ashes in the Garden of Remembrance.

Woman: No tricks? No jokes?

Undertaker: Indeed no. Unless you count… but it is a very small one.

Woman: A very small what?

Undertaker: A very small rollercoaster. Like the rest of the rides. Of course, we do have rather a large Haunted House.

Woman: More a Funfair of Remembrance, really. I don't think my uncle would have wanted that.

Undertaker: Was the deceased a little lacking in humour, perhaps?

Woman: You can say that again. He was a traffic warden, very zealous. Even gave me a ticket once!

Undertaker: Dear, dear.

Woman: I was picking my aunt up from the doctor's. His wife! She was on crutches at the time. And I was only giving her a lift because he was too mean to pay for a taxi.

They both stare at the urn.

Woman: Bastard.

Undertaker: Ex-bastard.

Woman: He didn't like Norman Wisdom, you know. Well, he didn't like any of them. Couldn't take a joke. He would have hated that funeral. Hated it. (*She smiles.*)

Undertaker: Modom is feeling better?

Woman: Oh, yes. Yes, indeed.

She laughs. The undertaker looks smug.

END

Sitcom – Chapters 9, 10 and 11

THE HOUSE OF RELAXATION by Lesley Bown and Ann Gawthorpe

Note: for performance we changed Laura's name to Eve and called the piece Adam 'n' Eve.

MOVING DAY

SCENE 1. INT DAY. THE RECEPTION AREA

Stuart is sitting cross-legged, meditating and reciting a mantra. Wendy enters carrying several box files. She drops the files on the desk, looks at Stuart. He doesn't react. She puts one CD in the computer and one CD in the sound system. Loud music blares out. Stuart leaps to his feet, turns off music.

STUART: That's like, you know, really really dangerous?

WENDY: If I was going to attack you, Stuart, I'd use something sharper than the Spice Girls.

Adam enters carrying cardboard box.

ADAM: Hey, people, where'd the music go?

WENDY: He doesn't like it.

ADAM: That's cool. Tell ya what, kid, run out and buy us some new sounds. Something really peppy and zippy.

STUART: You mean, like, the music from *Rainbow*?

ADAM: No, no, something, you know, young and zappy. Like us. Something nice and loud.

STUART: I don't think Laura will like that. She likes everything peaceful. (*Picks up CD from desk, reads label*) 'Birdsong in the rainforest'. We usually have that in the mornings. (*He puts the CD in the player.*)

FX: *twitterings*

ADAM: No no no no no. (*To Wendy*) Break out the Oasis, kiddo. Let's get some atmos in here.

STUART: No, that's no good, look, (*Picks up brochure from desk, reads*) 'The House of Relaxation is a haven of quiet in the midst of city turmoil'. Haven of quiet, right?

ADAM: Well now it's gonna be an oasis of, er, Oasis.

STUART: You can't do that. Supposing someone comes through the door, right, and their aura is all, like, ragged, and it needs smoothing out? You can't do that kind of thing with your head full of noise.

WENDY: This is never going to work, Adam. We can't share an office with a bunch of loonies, we just can't.

ADAM: I need to be here. Keep an eye on things. Aunty Margaret would have wanted it.

Laura enters, tragic.

LAURA: Did I hear someone say... Margaret? (*Sobs*)

STUART: Now look what you've done. (*To Laura*) Let it all out, OK? (*He passes her a box of tissues.*)

LAURA: Yes, yes, I must, mustn't I?

ADAM: Hey, we're all sad. She was my aunty, remember? I mean, you've only lost a business partner, I've lost family. Wendy, doughnuts, chop chop, there's a good girl.

WENDY: I keep telling you, I've a degree in computer science. I don't do cake shops.

LAURA: Still, it's not as if she's really gone.

ADAM: She's gone, believe me, I was at the funeral. So were you.

STUART: That's just, like, her old body? It's not important.

ADAM: Not to you maybe, sunshine, but she kind of needed it. Anyway, the business was getting too much for her.

LAURA: No it wasn't.

ADAM: That's why she left it to me. Someone young...

WENDY: Huh!

ADAM: ...someone energetic. Someone with a vision for the new Millennium!

STUART: Laura sees visions, don't you Laura?

LAURA: Sometimes, Stuart.

WENDY: I can see one right now. It's me down at the Job Centre.

LAURA: If only I knew why Margaret left her share to you, Adam. It seems so odd.

STUART: Why don't you ask her?

LAURA: I will, the next time we talk I'll ask her.

WENDY: Adam, I'm telling you, this stuff really freaks me out.

STUART: That's because you're resisting. If you just kind of relax, and sort of let yourself go...

Stuart starts to massage Wendy's shoulders. She pushes him away.

ADAM: Wendy doesn't ever let anything go, do you Wendy?

LAURA: Ah, a deep-seated need for control.

WENDY: A deep-seated need for a bit of common sense, thank you very much. I mean, I thought working for Adam was like taking a daily trip up the yellow brick road...

ADAM: You know, I gave you a job when you were desperate...

LAURA: Desperate? She's got a degree in computer science.

ADAM: Total Mickey Mouse. Correspondence course. She knows all there is to know about BBC computers for schools, 1985 vintage. Don't you, Wendy?

WENDY: When I first knew you, you were in the software Stone Age.

LAURA: I'm sensing a little bit of aggression here. Stuart, I think we need the grumpy hats.

Stuart takes bobble hats from a drawer, puts one on, starts handing out the others.

LAURA: Now, why don't we all form a circle and…

WENDY: Oh form your own circle. I've got work to do. (*She exits.*)

ADAM: Women, eh?

STUART: How do you mean, Adam?

LAURA: Oh, dear. I shall have take five minutes out to calm myself. I'll be in my room, Stuart. (*She exits to her room.*)

ADAM: That's what I mean. First sign of trouble and they're off. (*He exits to Laura's room.*)

FX: phone rings. Stuart answers it.

STUART: Hi, it's Stuart? How can I help? (*Looks in appointment book*) Sure, yeah, you can see a counsellor. Yeah, she's really nice. No, she never shouts. Really. Yeah, you can come today. What about… two 'o' clock? Is that cool for you? Give us your name, then. James? Oh, Mr Jamieson. All right, then. (*Writes in the book*)

SCENE 2. INT DAY. LAURA'S ROOM

ADAM: Feeling better? Good, lovely. Now, about my office. This room will do me fine.

LAURA: I don't know, that could be a little difficult. My work is confidential, you see. (*Adam picks up a crystal, fiddles with it.*)

ADAM: I don't mean us to share it, I mean you to move into the other room.

LAURA: But that's Margaret's room.

ADAM: Was. (*He puts the crystal in the wrong place.*)

LAURA: She's your aunt. She wants you to have it. (*She moves the crystal back.*)

ADAM: But you were so much closer to her than me. I haven't even seen her since I was fifteen. She turned up on my birthday with some Winnie the Pooh slippers.

LAURA: I really do have to have this room. (*Closes her eyes, puts hand on chest.*) This room speaks to me, somehow. It's, it's… on my wavelength. It's got something…

ADAM: A fabulous view and plenty of space? (*He moves one of the easy chairs.*) My desk could go here.

LAURA: (*opening eyes, glaring at Adam*) This is my room. (*She pushes the chair back into place.*) Besides, it would mean moving Stuart to the other side of the reception area, and he'd never do that.

ADAM: I think you're missing something here, Laura. You are his boss. That means, you tell him what to do, and then he does it.

LAURA: He's a Taurus. Very stubborn.

ADAM: I don't see why I should have that poky little room. We're equal partners.

LAURA: But Margaret liked that room.

ADAM: Well, I don't.

LAURA: Oh, this is too much. First I lose Margaret, then my room. (*She sobs dramatically.*)

Adam and Laura glare at each other. Stuart enters.

STUART: Adam, somebody on the phone for you?

Stuart exits. Adam looks exasperated, then exits. Laura rummages in her bag, desk, cupboard, etc. Pauses to think, lifts up statue of Buddha, finds key underneath.

SCENE 3. INT DAY. RECEPTION AREA

Adam is on the phone. Wendy is unpacking. Stuart is at his desk. Laura enters from her room. She locks the door behind her.

STUART: Oh no, locking the door, that's like, really bad karma? Like a prison or something?

LAURA: Try to think of it more as security. A safe place.

ADAM: Half-past nine, then. Excellent. (*He hangs up.*)

ADAM: Great. Now, Laura, about this little problem over rooms…

LAURA: I don't see a problem, Adam.

ADAM: You only see solutions? That's my kind of thinking.

STUART: No, she means defining something as a problem is a negative way of looking at it.

LAURA: That's right. You could look on this a chance for personal growth, Adam.

ADAM: If I grew I wouldn't fit in the room, would I?

LAURA: I'm sure you'll cope wonderfully. Now, anyone want anything from the garden centre?

WENDY: You're going shopping? I thought your heart was broken?

LAURA: I'll feel better if I go.

ADAM: Shopping for grief therapy? Could be an interesting new marketing concept there.

STUART: No, she's going to find Margaret.

ADAM: At the garden centre?

WENDY: Margaret is dead, you know that.

STUART: Reincarnation. She told us she was sure she'd come back as a tree. We're going to plant her somewhere beautiful.

Laura exits.

ADAM: Damn, I should have asked her to pick up the doughnuts. Wendy…

WENDY: No.

ADAM: This is crazy. Stuart, if Laura asked you to get doughnuts, you would, wouldn't you?

STUART: No way.

WENDY: See?

STUART: White sugar is really really bad for you? I might get her carrot cake. She likes carrot cake.

ADAM: OK, just this once, I will get the doughnuts. And if my new client turns up, Wendy, if it's not too much trouble, would you show him through to the office and get him a coffee?

WENDY: No.

ADAM: You've always done the coffee. You can't move the goalposts just like that.

WENDY: It's not that. They haven't got any.

ADAM: No coffee?

Stuart shakes his head.

WENDY: Not allowed. Bad for us apparently.

ADAM: Bad for you, coffee? Well I practically live off the stuff and I'm pretty normal, hey guys?

STUART: I could rustle up a nice camomile tea. Very soothing.

ADAM: Never mind. Just look after him. He's coming to consult the Millennium Maestro.

STUART: Wow, is that a new therapy?

ADAM: No, it's marketing. This is a brand new Millennium, Stuart. Every business in the land needs a Millennium angle. And I'm the guy to do it. I help them maximize their Millennium marketing potential.

Stuart looks puzzled.

WENDY: He means T-shirts. He puts the company name on T-shirts and calls that a Millennium angle. That's all.

ADAM: That is not all, not by a very long shot.

WENDY: OK, so he does biros as well.

ADAM: Well now we're doing shopping trolleys, or will be if we land the account. The publicity potential of the shopping trolley has barely been scratched.

STUART: I'll put him in the book, then. (*Opens appointment book*) See, I've done a special column for your appointments, with a lilac line, because you're a lilac kind of person, OK Adam?

ADAM: No it is not OK. For a start, I'm red. Definitely red. Very red. (*Rummages in box, produces electronic organizer*) And all my appointments are in here. Wendy, I'll be busy all morning with this guy. (*Passes her the organizer*)

WENDY: This is the twenty-first century, Stuart. (*She presses buttons.*)

VOICE: You have no free time this morning. Have a nice day.

STUART: Wow.

Adam takes organizer, puts it on desk next to appointment book. He exits.

WENDY: Where's the kettle?

STUART: (*pointing*) In the kitchen. And the camomile tea is on the shelf.

WENDY: I won't be needing that, thank you very much.

She exits to kitchen. Stuart looks at organizer, his hand hovers towards it.

FX: phone rings. Stuart answers it.

STUART: Hi it's Stuart? (*Beat*) This morning? Er, are you sure you need to come twice in one day? That is Mr Jamieson, isn't it? (*Looks in book*) I've already got you in for two 'o' clock. No don't worry, it's easily done. Like I'm always turning up for work on a Sunday? Yeah, right. 'Bye.

Stuart hangs up, turns back to organizer. Wendy enters with cup of hot water. He snatches his hand back.

STUART: Find it all right, then?

WENDY: It was a challenge, but I managed. (*She takes a jar of coffee from her bag, opens it, sniffs the aroma.*)

STUART: That's coffee!

WENDY: So it is. (*She spoons some into her cup, stirs and inhales.*)

WENDY: Mmm, lovely. Bet you want some, don't you Stuart?

STUART: No. And you told Adam, you said there wasn't any coffee.

WENDY: No I didn't. I said I wouldn't make coffee for his client, and I said coffee wasn't allowed in here.

STUART: You know what I mean.

WENDY: This is my own personal coffee, which I paid for myself. If Adam wants coffee, he can get his own. (*She raises the cup to her lips, sips.*)

Adam enters with doughnuts, Wendy splutters and hides cup beneath her desk.

ADAM: I can smell coffee!

STUART: She's got coffee. Under her desk.

WENDY: Tell tale!

ADAM: Ah, I knew she'd look after me. Coffee, Wendy, please, I'll be in my office – and don't forget my client. (*He takes a doughnut, drops the bag on Wendy's desk, exits to his room. Wendy picks up coffee jar and exits to the kitchen. Stuart touches the organizer.*)

VOICE: You have no free time this morning. Have a nice day.

Wendy looks out of kitchen.

WENDY: Leave that alone! You haven't been trained to use it.

STUART: Sorry.

WENDY: Don't you touch it again. (*She disappears to kitchen briefly, enters with cup of coffee, crosses to Adam's room, knocks, opens door.*)

FX: *phone on Wendy's desk rings.*

Before Stuart can answer it, Wendy exits from Adam's room and answers the phone.

WENDY: Millennium Maestro. Ah, good morning. Yes. Yes. Of course, no problem. (*She hangs up. presses buttons on organizer, crosses to Adam's office, knocks and enters.*)

SCENE 4. INT DAY. ADAM'S OFFICE

WENDY: I just had your new client on the phone, Adam. He's rearranged for this afternoon, about one-thirty.

ADAM: Okey-dokey. (*Leans back in chair*) Maybe I'll just catch some zeds.

WENDY: We've still got a lot of stuff at the old office, Adam.

ADAM: Yeah. (*Takes car keys from pocket*) Tell you what, how'd you like to do it?

WENDY: No thanks.

ADAM: (*Holds out keys*) You'll get to drive the beamer.

WENDY: I don't do removals.

ADAM: Why aren't I surprised? OK, I'll drive, but will you come and help? If it's not too much trouble, of course.

WENDY: I don't know.

ADAM: Lunch is on me?

WENDY: Oh, all right.

SCENE 5. INT DAY. RECEPTION AREA

Adam and Wendy enter from Adam's office.

ADAM: Hey, Stuart, kiddo, howja like to be in charge for a bit?

STUART: Oh, no. Power corrupts, you know.

Wendy picks up piece of paper and pencil.

WENDY: Just answer the phone and write down our messages. And don't touch that. (*Points to the organizer*)

Adam and Wendy exit. Stuart hovers over organizer.

STUART: It's like, covered in little buttons? (*He reaches out, and snatches his hand back.*) I bet it takes loads of training. Months and months. (*He touches the organizer*) It can't be that hard. (*He presses a button.*)

VOICE: You have no free time this morning.

STUART: Wow. It's just so easy. (*He touches another button.*)

VOICE: Mr Jamieson is due at thirteen thirty hours.

STUART: Oh, wow, how did you know that? But you got the time wrong, you know? (*He presses buttons.*) I just spoke to him on the phone, right? He's coming at two.

VOICE: It is three twenty-nine pm.

STUART: No it isn't. (*He presses another button.*)

VOICE: It is your wife's birthday tomorrow. You are due for a dental check up. Mind the doors please.

Stuart frantically presses buttons, nothing happens. Laura enters, carrying odd-looking pot plant. Puts it on desk with great reverence.

LAURA: (*brokenly*) Oh, Margaret!

STUART: Oh, crumbs.

SCENE 6. INT DAY. RECEPTION AREA. CLOCK SHOWS 1.30

Laura is fussing over the plant. Wendy enters carrying box of files.

WENDY: Ugh, what's that?

LAURA: It's Margaret.

WENDY: You said she was coming back as a tree.

LAURA: It's what she wants. I felt it as soon as I got into the garden centre. I was heading for the trees but I felt myself being sort of pulled, pulled…

WENDY: You probably got one of those trolleys with wonky wheels.

LAURA: She wants to be near us. (*To plant*) You do, don't you? She doesn't want to be planted out in some cold lonely field. This way is nicer.

WENDY: And cheaper. Well, keep it away from me, I'm allergic to the nasty things. (*She sneezes*)

LAURA: You should try to bond with her. Female solidarity is so important, don't you think dear?

WENDY: I am not bonding with a pot plant, however female it is.

LAURA: I used to look up to Margaret, you know. She was a mother figure to me, with so much wisdom. I feel that I could do the same for you, somehow.

WENDY: I've already got a mother, thank you very much.

LAURA: I could give you so much advice. Men, for instance. I sense that your manner puts them off. Men like a women to be soft. Feminine.

WENDY: Now you do sound like my mother.

LAURA: And, of course, however desperate you are, you must never let it show.

WENDY: I'm not desperate, I've got loads of boyfriends, actually, loads.

LAURA: There's nothing wrong with being a single woman, Wendy. Look at me, I'm perfectly happy and fulfilled. I can be a role model for you.

WENDY: But you're heaps older than me!

LAURA: Not that much, dear. Although I do have an instinct for handling men. Take Adam, for instance. He's inclined to be a little bit dominant, don't you find?

WENDY: I'm not even thirty yet. Not for ages.

LAURA: That's why we can't let him have my room, do you see?

Stuart enters with plant sprayer.

STUART: Look what I've bought for Margaret!

LAURA: Just remember what I said. We must stick together, mustn't we?

STUART: Where shall we put her?

WENDY: Get rid of it, for goodness sake.

LAURA: But this is where she needs to be. Margaret needs to be among us.

STUART: Oh yes, she'll have to be here with us.

WENDY: Well if she comes over here she'll get pruned.

Laura and Stuart look at each other.

STUART: Look at that aura.

LAURA: Mmm, I know. Grumpy hat I think, Stuart.

Stuart pulls out bobble hats.

WENDY: Whatever game this is, I'm not playing.

LAURA: So much negative energy. I'm sure we can help you.

WENDY: Please don't.

STUART: But we always do this. Look, (*pulls on a hat*) see, when I'm wearing the hat, I'm taking time out from my anger.

LAURA: Margaret and I always worked through our issues wearing our hats. When you take the hat off, you leave your issues behind you, in the hat. (*She puts on a hat.*)

Wendy throws her hat in waste-paper basket.

WENDY: What you two weirdoes get up to is your business. (*Picks up papers*) If you'll excuse me, I've got photocopying to do. (*She exits.*)

LAURA: Poor girl.

Laura removes hat and exits to her room. Stuart keeps his hat on. Stuart goes to the organizer and starts punching buttons.

STUART: Hi, this is Stuart? Um, are you still feeling a bit confused?

VOICE: You weigh eleven stone. You have aggressive tendencies.

STUART: That's just so wrong. (*Shakes the organizer*)

VOICE: Instruction accepted. All data has been removed.

STUART: Oh, no, oh, no, I've broken it! (*Puts his hand to his chest, pants*) I'm having a panic attack! Paper bag! Paper bag! (*He sees the bag of doughnuts, picks it up, takes out one doughnut, looks round.*) Plate! Plate! (*He exits to the kitchen.*)

A man, harassed, enters, talking on mobile phone

MAN: ...now listen to me laddie, it's time you bucked up your ideas. (*Beat*) Don't give me that. I'm just about to see this marketing consultant and I'll be back at the works in 45 minutes. I expect to find you there bright-eyed and bushy tailed and wearing your overalls. (*Beat*) I don't care if you have got an appointment with a counsellor. It's all nonsense. You cancel it and get on with some hard work, you hear me? (*Hangs up phone*)

Stuart enters from the kitchen carrying doughnuts on a plate. He has sugar and jam all over his face.

MAN: I don't know what you lads are coming to.

STUART: I'm sorry?

MAN: Confused, he says. Needs to sort his head out, he says.

STUART: Aah.

MAN: Now don't you take his side.

STUART: OK.

Silence. Man glares at Stuart.

MAN: I don't want to be a nuisance or possibly even force you to do your job, but I do have an appointment. If it's not too much trouble.

Stuart looks at organizer.

STUART: Who with?

MAN: Well, whoever it is in this organization that sorts out problems.

Stuart looks in the book.

STUART: Er... Mr Jamieson?

MAN: That's me.

STUART: Come this way, please. (*He knocks on Laura's door and opens it.*)

STUART: Mr Jamieson is here, Laura.

MAN: Wash your face, laddie, it's covered in your lunch.

Man exits to Laura's room. Adam enters carrying box of files. Stuart is wiping his face with a tissue.

ADAM: Everything OK, Stuart?

STUART: Er, well...

ADAM: That's the way. (*Sees plant*) What's that monstrosity?

STUART: That's your aunty, Adam.

ADAM: She never was much of a looker. Where's Wendy?

STUART: Gone down to the photocopier.

ADAM: That's a good sign. It means she's settling in. Stuart?

STUART: Yes, Adam?

ADAM: Look, since it's just us guys together, can I speak frankly?

STUART: OK.

ADAM: Well, I think Wendy would settle even better if she had her desk over there.

STUART: It would be very crowded with two of us. And that side would be empty.

ADAM: True. Well, maybe we could move your desk to where hers is now?

STUART: But this is my side, I meditate on this side. No, it wouldn't work. Sorry.

ADAM: It's just that I don't like to see Wendy upset. I have a bit of a soft spot where girls are concerned, Stuart. You know how it is. I can't bear the tears.

STUART: She makes you cry, does she?

ADAM: No, Wendy's tears. You don't think I cry, do you?

STUART: Crying is healthy for us all, Adam. Actually, Wendy strikes me as someone who doesn't cry enough. She keeps it all bottled up inside. That's not good.

ADAM: OK. Well you can be the one to tell her. Let's see how you like that. Now if my client turns up Stuart, I don't suppose you'd make him a cup of... no, never mind. Just show him through, would you? (*He exits to his room.*)

SCENE 7. INT DAY. LAURA'S ROOM

Laura and the man are facing each other across a low table.

MAN: I didn't expect to be seeing a lass.

LAURA: Does that bother you?

MAN: Not if you know your stuff. Well, fire away.

LAURA: Hmmm. Is there anything you want to tell me?

MAN: How do you mean?

LAURA: I mean whatever you want me to mean.

MAN: Oh, ha, very clever, get me to do all the work, eh, I tell you what I want?

LAURA: Only if you want to.

MAN: Well, OK, I'll play your little game. I want a plan, that's what I want, I want it simple, I want it straightforward and I don't want it to cost too much.

LAURA: I see.

MAN: The question is, can you deliver? I'm not looking for some airy fairy, arty farty nonsense. As far as I'm concerned, a trolley is a trolley.

LAURA: I see. You see a trolley as a metaphor for life?

MAN: If it steers straight, I'm a happy man.

LAURA: And does it? Does your trolley steer straight?

SCENE 8. INT DAY. THE RECEPTION AREA

Stuart is at the desk. Wendy enters carrying pile of photocopying.

WENDY: Stuart, would you say I looked desperate?

STUART: Oh no, you look very nice. Why?

WENDY: Never mind.

STUART: By the way Wendy, I have something to tell you. (*He has the box of tissues ready*.)

WENDY: What?

STUART: I'm afraid it won't be possible for you to move your desk over here. (*He pushes the tissues towards her*.)

WENDY: OK.

STUART: I have to have my desk over here. I need to meditate, and I need to sit here, where the vibes are right, do you see?

WENDY: No.

STUART: Well I do just have to sit here. How do you feel about that?

WENDY: Fine.

STUART: Adam thought you might cry.

WENDY: Oh no. I never cry. I just get revenge.

A scruffy young man enters.

WENDY: Can I help you?

YOUNG MAN: I've got an appointment. I think.

WENDY: You don't think I look desperate, do you?

YOUNG MAN: Oh, have we started?

WENDY: Forget it. (*She presses organizer*.)

VOICE: You have no appointments.

WENDY: That can't be right.

Stuart looks in the book.

STUART: I've got a Mrs Hudson, but that's tomorrow.

WENDY: (*pressing buttons*) Somebody's been messing around with this.

YOUNG MAN: I'm not Mrs Hudson. I think.

STUART: It was me. Sorry.

YOUNG MAN: You're Mrs Hudson?

STUART: No, I'm Stuart.

YOUNG MAN: Perhaps I thought I was Mrs Hudson when I made the call. I do get confused.

WENDY: Why can't you just leave things alone?

YOUNG MAN: Sorry.

WENDY: Not you. Him.

YOUNG MAN: Sorry.

STUART: I'm really, really sorry, Wendy. I'll do anything to make it up to you.

WENDY: Fine. There's still plenty of stuff in the boot of Adam's car. Off you go.

Young man starts to exit. Wendy holds up her hand to stop him. Stuart exits. Adam enters from his room.

ADAM: Ah, good afternoon, Mr Jamieson?

YOUNG MAN: Er... possibly.

Adam shakes him vigorously by the hand.

ADAM: Let me say at once you've come to the right place. We can solve all your problems.

YOUNG MAN: Oh, good.

ADAM: You sounded older on the phone. One of our younger entrepreneurs, eh?

YOUNG MAN: Probably.

ADAM: Shall I take your, er, anorak? (*He takes it and hangs it up*) Well, if you'd like to go in. Make yourself comfortable.

Young man exits to Adam's room. Adam crosses to Wendy.

ADAM: I want you to get your desk over that side.

WENDY: I know.

ADAM: Use your feminine wiles on Stuart. He'll be a pushover.

WENDY: Perhaps you'd like me to sleep with him? Apparently I'm desperate.

ADAM: No need to go over the top. A few tears should do the trick.

SCENE 9. INT DAY. LAURA'S ROOM

The businessman is leaning back in his chair, tie undone.

LAURA: So what would you say was the real problem here?

MAN: It all started with the Millennium.

LAURA: Mmm. A lot of people were worried about that.

MAN: Well, of course. For a start, there was the bug.

LAURA: You're worried about a bug?

MAN: I handed the whole thing over to the boy. You see, I wanted him to take some responsibility for once. It didn't work. Gormless, that's what he is. My own son.

LAURA: I see.

MAN: I said to him, I said, it's the Millennium. You'll have to shape up, laddie. Ask yourself, what does it mean? Where are we going?

LAURA: Those are big questions.

MAN: Aye, but they have to be answered. I said to the boy, we're standing still, we can't afford to stand still. There's no standing still in the world of trolleys.

LAURA: Because of the wheels?

SCENE 10. INT DAY. ADAM'S ROOM

The young man is sitting on the couch, surrounded by cardboard boxes.

ADAM: … and if you follow me so far, it's a simple question of setting up a cost-benefit analysis and transferring the results into a reality-based action plan.

YOUNG MAN: Do you mind if I lie down?

ADAM: Well, no, you go ahead.

The young man stretches out on the couch among the boxes.

YOUNG MAN: I'm afraid I'm not very good at action. A bit indecisive.

ADAM: And that's why you need me. I can make it all perfectly simple and smooth for you.

YOUNG MAN: Oh, good.

ADAM: We ought to start by identifying the problem and breaking it down into a series of core components.

YOUNG MAN: It all started with the Millennium.

ADAM: I know.

YOUNG MAN: I knew you would. You make me feel, somehow… safe.

ADAM: It's a simple question of prioritizing.

YOUNG MAN: I don't know. It was all so uncertain. People couldn't even agree on the date, you know. We could still be heading for Armageddon.

ADAM: Out-of-town shopping centre? Perfect.

YOUNG MAN: It could be the end of the world as we know it.

ADAM: Oh yes. It's the start of a wonderful new world.

YOUNG MAN: Is it?

SCENE 11. INT DAY. LAURA'S ROOM

The man is lying on the couch, shoes off. Laura is giving him reflexology.

MAN: Oh, ah, mmm.

LAURA: That's better, isn't it?

MAN: That's wonderful. Just wonderful.

LAURA: No more worrying about the Millennium?

MAN: Oh no.

LAURA: No more worrying about your son?

MAN: Oh no. He's a good boy. Sorry, I mean young man.

LAURA: That's right.

MAN: It's not his fault he doesn't like the trolleys.

LAURA: No, indeed.

SCENE 12. INT DAY. ADAM'S ROOM

Adam is squashed in the corner, standing by a flip chart with complicated diagrams. The young man is watching from the couch, from behind a wall of boxes.

ADAM: So, if we follow the demand curve to here, taking account of the profitability axis, what do we get?

YOUNG MAN: *(panicky)* I don't know, I don't know.

ADAM: T-shirts, right? We get T-shirts.

YOUNG MAN: T-shirts? Not biros?

ADAM: You're beginning to get the hang of this.

SCENE 13. INT DAY. RECEPTION AREA

Wendy and Stuart are at their desks.

WENDY: So, tell me, Stuart, what do you do in your spare time?

STUART: Oh, you know. The usual.

WENDY: The usual what?

STUART: Oh, you know. Yoga. T'ai Chi. And Laura wants me to go to assertiveness.

WENDY: Just a normal regular guy, then?

STUART: Yes.

WENDY: And do you really believe all this stuff?

STUART: All what stuff?

WENDY: Oh, auras and karma and coming back as a tatty pot plant.

STUART: Of course I do. In fact, reading auras is, like, my speciality?

WENDY: So, what happened to Margaret's aura? Does it stay with her? Has her plant got it?

STUART: I don't know. She doesn't seem to be on my wavelength.

WENDY: Oh, dear.

STUART: Laura can always make contact.

WENDY: The thing is Stuart, er, how does it come through? Do you hear voices in your head?

STUART: Oh no, nothing like that. Laura says she just gets a sort of feeling, and somehow she knows what the person wants.

WENDY: That might explain it...

STUART: What? Can you hear Margaret? Can you?

WENDY: Well, I'm not sure. I just get this feeling (*picks up plant*) that I have to move it, er, her, over to this side (*walks across*) oh, no (*stops near her desk*) now I'm getting a feeling... that she doesn't want to upset anyone. What can it mean?

STUART: (*excited*) She wants to be on your desk, it must be that.

WENDY: But then, what about that other feeling? Just when I got next to my desk... I can't explain it. Help me Stuart.

STUART: (*bitterly*) I don't know. Why should she talk to you? She never even met you. It's not fair.

WENDY: (*fakes a sneeze*) I know, it's my allergy. She doesn't want to set it off. Was she a very caring person, Stuart?

STUART: I suppose.

WENDY: Look, let's try something. Come and stand here. (*She leads him to her desk, puts the plant in his hand*) Oh yes, that's better. She likes that. But it's still not quite right. Here, try this. (*She gives Stuart the appointment book, and moves across to Stuart's desk. They have now changed places*) That's it! Oh Stuart, she loves being over there with you.

SCENE 14. INT DAY. ADAM'S ROOM

The young man is standing up, excited. Adam is sitting on the couch.

YOUNG MAN: So what you're saying is, the aim of the game is to make money?

ADAM: Now we're cooking with gas!

YOUNG MAN: And when you've made it, you can spend it?

ADAM: Whatever you want. Fast car, penthouse flat. New anorak.

YOUNG MAN: My dad says it's all about getting up early and shouting at people.

ADAM: Nah, that's the old way. I'm showing you the bright new shiny Millennium way. Together we can make a fortune.

YOUNG MAN: Oh, I won't be needing you. (*Holds out hand*) I'll be off then. Cheerio. (*He exits.*)

ADAM: Hang on, wait... (*He exits.*)

SCENE 15. INT DAY. RECEPTION AREA

Wendy is working at Stuart's desk. Stuart has the plant on Wendy's desk. The young man is putting on his anorak. Adam enters.

ADAM: Right, when shall we meet again?

YOUNG MAN: Look, I just told you. I can do this on my own.

ADAM: But I've got the marketing expertise...

YOUNG MAN: It seems perfectly simple to me. I'm not paying you to run up a few T-shirts. I'm going to need all my money, aren't I, eh? There's the anorak for a start, that won't come cheap.

ADAM: Shall I pencil you in for Wednesday? Wendy, check if I've got a window on Wednesday, would you?

The man enters from Laura's room, followed by Laura. He is holding a flower.

MAN: Can I come again? Next week?

LAURA: Of course you can. Whenever you want.

YOUNG MAN: Dad! What are you doing here?

MAN: My boy! (*He embraces the young man tearfully.*)

YOUNG MAN: (*pushing him away*) That's enough of that.

MAN: No, you don't understand. When I came here I thought I was going to see a marketing consultant...

ADAM: He's my client!

MAN: ...but now I see that none of that matters.

ADAM: (*to Laura*) You stole my client!

LAURA: I did not. He found me.

MAN: I've been too hard on you, son. Can you forgive me?

ADAM: (*to man*) Look, why don't you come into my office, and we can get to grips with this thing.

YOUNG MAN: (*to man*) I haven't got time for this right now, dad. But we must meet up soon. Why don't we do lunch? Give me a call, OK? Ciao. (*He exits.*)

ADAM: (*to man*) I'm afraid there's been a bit of a mix-up. I can't think how.

MAN: Never mind, it doesn't matter. (*He gives Adam the flower.*) (*To Laura*) I'll see you next week, my dear.

ADAM: No!

Man exits.

LAURA: Things always turn out for the best Adam, if you let them.

ADAM: No, they don't. Somewhere along the line I've lost the chance to make a pot of money.

LAURA: Oh, Adam, money isn't important. Possessions aren't important. You'll come to see that one day. (*She turns towards her room.*)

ADAM: Hang on, hang on. I think I'll be having that room after all.

LAURA: What makes you think that?

ADAM: Look. Wendy and Stuart have swapped. So now it makes sense for us to swap. It's only a room, Laura. Possessions aren't important.

LAURA: Stuart, what on earth were you thinking of?

STUART: It wasn't me. It was Margaret.

LAURA: What?

ADAM: Oh aunty, thank you.

WENDY: Yes I'm sorry Laura, Margaret told me she wanted to be on this side. And of course, with my allergy, well, you know, I'm desperate not to set it off.

LAURA: Allergy? Hah!

WENDY: I'm sensing a bit of aggression here. Hat, Stuart, quick.

STUART: (*claps his hands*) Cool.

Stuart pulls out bobble hats, gives one to Laura who tosses it aside, and one to Wendy.

ADAM: (*to Laura*) So, I'll start moving my stuff. Key, please.

Stuart gives him a hat, he looks puzzled, but puts it on.

LAURA: (*to Wendy*) I thought we bonded. Women should be able to resolve their issues, Wendy.

STUART: Put yours on, Wendy.

WENDY: Oh no, not me. (*She puts the hat over the plant.*) Resolve it with her.

END

Appendix G:
Taking it further

Books on comedy writing

Ashton, Brad, *How to Write Comedy* (Hamish Hamilton, 1983)

Byrne, John, *Writing Comedy*, 3rd edn (A & C Black, 2005)

Byrne, John and Powell, Marcus, *Writing Sitcoms* (A & C Black, 2003)

Helitzer, Mel with Shatz, Mark, *Comedy Writing Secrets* (Writer's Digest Books, 2005). Highly recommended, although aimed at the American market

Perret, Gene, *Comedy Writing Step by Step,* revised edn (Quill Driver Books, 2007). Highly recommended, although aimed at the American market

Wolfe, Ronald, *Writing Comedy*, revised edn (Robert Hale, 2003)

General guidance

Writers' & Artists' Yearbook (A & C Black)

The Writers' Handbook (Pan McMillan)

Partridge, Eric, *Usage and Abusage* (Book Club Associates, 1980)

Room, Adrian, *Dictionary of Confusibles* (Routledge & Kegan Paul, 1979)

Fieldhouse, Harry, *Everyman's Good English Guide* (J.M. Dent, 1982)

New Oxford Style Manual (Oxford University Press, 2012)

Gowers, Ernest, Greenbaum, Sidney and Whitcut, Janet, *The Complete Plain Words* (HMSO, 2004)

DVDs

Rowan Atkinson's excellent series on comedy, known as both *Funny Business* and *Laughing Matters,* is available on DVD but can be hard to track down.

Courses

Mindy Glazer's Sitcom Writing Course

Mindy Glazer currently teaches sitcom writing on ed2go.com, the largest purveyor of online classes in the English-speaking world. She wrote for *Who's the Boss, Kate and Allie* and *My Two Dads*, among other shows. She is also the author of three novels and many non-fiction, magazine and newspaper pieces. Her class 'Breaking Into Sitcom Writing' was among the first college-level sitcom-writing classes.

http://www.ed2go.com/CourseDetails.aspx?query=sitcom+writing&course=bsw&tab=detail

Arvon

Short residential courses including specific comedy writing courses: /http://www.arvon.org

National Writers' Centre for Wales

Week-long residential writing courses, not specifically about comedy: http://www.tynewydd.org

Swanwick Summer School

Week-long residential courses in Swanwick near Derby. Check programme for comedy: http://www.swanwickwritersschool.org.uk

Southampton Solent University: BA (Hons) Comedy – Writing and Performance (full time)

http://www.solent.ac.uk/courses/undergraduate/comedy_writing_and_performance_ba/course_details.aspx

East Park Terrace

Southampton

Hampshire

SO14 0YN

Telephone: +44 (0)23 8031 9039

Email: ask@solent.ac.ukl

Introduction to Comedy Writing

www.racc.ac.uk/

Richmond Adult Community College

Parkshot
Richmond TW9 2RE

General enquiries: 020 8891 5907

Email Info:racc.ac.uk

Magazines

Writers' Forum, monthly: http://www.writers-forum.com/

Writing Magazine, monthly. Subscribers also receive *Writers' News*: http://www.writersnews.co.uk/

Organizations

Society of Authors: http://www.societyofauthors.net

The Writers' Guild of Great Britain: http://www.writersguild.org.uk

The Authors' Licensing and Collecting Society: www.alcs.co.uk

Able to remunerate authors with secondary royalties via collective licensing schemes from photocopying, etc.

Public Lending Right: www.plr.uk.com

Administered by Public Lending Right based in Stockton-upon-Tees and funded by the Department of Culture, Media and Sport (DCMS).

British Society of Comedy Writers: http://www.bscw.co.uk

Funny Women: www.funnywomen.com

Funny Women Ltd

St David's House 15

Worple Way

Richmond-upon-Thames

TW10 6DG

Office 020 8948 4444

Mobile 07973 470577

Lynne Parker, Producer: 'Through Funny Women, we actively encourage all aspects of female comedy and recognize that writing is as important as performing.' Runs workshops to encourage writing skills as much as performance and partners aspiring writers with performers who need to collaborate on material. Coaches performers and offers a platform for performance through the Funny Women Awards and regular showcases around the UK.

Websites

Two websites where you can self-publish at no cost, or pay a small amount for extra services:

- Createspace: www.createspace.com/
- Lulu: www.lulu.com

A comprehensive website including help and information for comedy writers: The British Comedy Guide www.comedy.co.uk/

American site for all types of writing: *Writer's Digest* www.writersdigest.com

Useful advice on writing for television: *Royal Television Society* www.rts.org.uk

For all information on writing for the BBC: The Writer's Room *at the BBC* www.bbc.co.uk/writersroom

Help with grammar: www.bbc.co.uk/skillswise/words/grammar/punctuation/commas/factsheet.shtml

The *Guardian* writing website has comedy writing contributions from Richard Herring and Catherine Tate: www.guardian.co.uk/books/series/howtowrite

Starting a blog:

- www.wordpress.com/
- www.blogger.com/home

Newsjack writers' guide: www.bbc.co.uk/programmes/b00kvs8r

Posting a novel online: Authonomy, run by HarperCollins, has a separate section for comedy www.authonomy.com/ Post your work and get feedback from other writers.

Copyright information: www.patent.gov.uk

Index